MW01123803

UNDER THE DOVE

UNDER THE DOVE

A COLLECTION OF MEMORIES

Lynne Lang

Imagine That Enterprises, L.C.
St. Louis, Missouri

Great care has been taken to accurately represent all parties in this publication. The author claims no responsibility for errors or omissions, but extends deepest apologies if that has occurred.

Printed in Canada.

Design and layout by Diane M. Beasley
Front cover photograph of Dove, Courtesy Philadelphia Sign Company
Front cover inside flap photograph of Dove taken down for refurbishment, 2001,
Courtesy Westfield Shoppingtown West County
Back cover photograph of Dove at Christmas,
Courtesy Westfield Shoppingtown West County
Back cover inside flap photograph of author by Dove during refurbishment,
Photo by Gary Lang

Library of Congress Control Number: 2002110674
Lang, Lynne
Under the Dove / Lynne Lang—1st ed.
ISBN 0-9723067-0-6
I. Under the Dove I. Title
2002

To order, contact Lynne Lang, P. O. Box 29315, St. Louis, MO 63126
www.underthedove.com

DB/DB/F

5 4 3 2

Foreword

Since 1969, the Dove has been soaring high over the City of Des Peres. Through the years, the Dove has served many roles – meeting spot, regional landmark, and a symbol of peaceful growth to the West.

Now, as a new Westfield Shoppingtown West County prepares to open, the Dove is reintroduced to the Des Peres skyline where it will continue to greet the community well into the future. To commemorate this occasion, please join us in taking a look at the Dove's rich history. In this book, we celebrate the traditions and stories behind this beloved symbol in West St. Louis County.

Westfield Shoppingtown West County is proud to serve you by providing exceptional customer service, quality retail, and a strong commitment to our community. With you, we take pride in West County and will continue the many civic efforts that have become tradition. As the Dove symbolizes, Westfield Shoppingtown West County is dedicated to serving the community by preserving the past and working toward a successful future.

Thank you for joining us in this grand celebration.

Scot Vallee, General Manager
Westfield Shoppingtown West County

My mother has been one of my biggest cheerleaders for as long as I can remember. She still sees potential in me beyond what I imagine for myself.

•

Mom, I hope I have your energy for living in the many years that lie ahead!

Preface

The journey of a thousand miles begins with a single step.
Confucius

Teens in the late 1960's may remember reading *Prom Magazine* while eating fries dripping in ketchup and sipping cherry sodas at the Woolworth counter. Friday evenings may have found these same teens cruising around town in cars with the windows rolled down, releasing the sounds of radios blasting into the warm, humid St. Louis air. As they chattered about their plans for Friday nights or summer excursions, the conversation usually ended with, "Let's just meet under the Dove." No one ever disputed that plan.

Today in 2002, F.W. Woolworth and *Prom Magazine* are lingering memories, but the Dove has survived the test of time. Today, just as we did in the late 1960's, thousands of St. Louisans use it as a landmark for giving directions to many destinations, or use it as a meeting place to connect before going elsewhere. It was convenient and an easily recognizable landmark. It was always easiest to meet under the Dove – everyone knew where it was!

Just as in the late 1960's, today this landmark continues to be significant in our lives. Our world is filled with change. The Dove has been with us for more than 30 years and links the past and the present. It arouses a bit of nostalgia for yesterday's generation and provides memories that seem very similar to those of young people today.

Why do doves seem so endearing? The dove has been a cherished symbol since biblical times. Noah was relieved and filled with hope when he released a dove and it returned bearing an olive branch. He had been on the ark for 40 days and nights during the floods that enveloped the earth, and now the dove brought news of dry land ahead. Abraham began selling doves in Jewish temples for use as sacrificial offerings. In the New Testament, Christians uphold the belief that the dove is a symbol for the Holy Spirit.

The author visited the Dove during renovation at Signcrafters, Inc.
Photo by Gary Lang

For centuries people have written about the dove's melancholy coo, the metallic luster of its plumage, and the beauty of its swift flight in flocks. With dark eyes encircled by a line of bright skin, their gentleness and innocence make doves a fitting symbol for trust, love, and peace.

In the 1960's during the Vietnam War the dove was a prominent sign of peace for a country torn between defending our overseas allies and protecting our own citizens here at home. Protesters did not want America involved in someone else's civil war, especially a war with no immediate end in sight.

A few Native American tribes use "prayer feathers," indicating that birds are spiritual beings because they fly high up into the sky, lifting prayer to the heavens. Other tribes believe feathers are sacred and should not touch the ground, as this symbolizes a fallen warrior. Some find it customary to release doves after a prayer ceremony. A good example might be the release of doves after weddings to symbolize the hope of two joining as one and beginning a new journey together.

The regional landmark that hovered over the western corner of what was formerly known as West County Center was nearly as recognizable as the St. Louis Arch! It seemed as though a piece of the sky was missing when the Dove was removed in February 2001. As the new center was under construction, I would drive by the spot where the Dove was perched, wondering if anyone had ever thought about collecting stories from St. Louisans about this symbol of peaceful prosperity. Each time I mentioned my curiosity about the memories people might have to share, family and friends would reply, "What a great idea – you should write a book about it!"

As I began to write this book, I discovered that many subplots or themes were emerging in my personal life, as well as in the book. My main goal for the book was to gather as many interviews and stories as I could while also managing my schedule with work, family, and friends. To my surprise, these subplots were essential to the main goal.

For instance, in my personal life I knew I was planning a wedding for our oldest daughter, but I planned my deadlines for the book around that. So my book project was punctuated with small and big diversions involving Rachel's wedding.

I also work full-time with students around the St. Louis area as a Health Educator for BJC HealthCare School Outreach and Youth Development. My students made the landscape of this project richer with their perspective. I have even included a few stories from them.

The most challenging subplot, however, was discovering that our oldest son was diagnosed with cancer just before I began writing this book. He returned home from college to receive care, without completing his final semester before graduating. This happened shortly after Westfield gave approval for the book project. Despite what might have been considered a major setback in my personal life, Westfield unknowingly provided the support necessary to move ahead with the book. They helped with publicity to gather stories and provided contacts to complete the history.

While these subplots have offered diversions from my work, they have also given perspective to what matters most. Having the support of my family and friends has made success not merely possible, but inevitable. This project took on a life of its own from the moment I began to talk about my idea. Events that happened became part of the weave of personal experiences, book interviews, and life in my everyday work world.

Author to write book about 'dove'

Lynne Lang seeks anecdotes, photos of historic West County landmark

By Jennifer Pope
Staff writer

Anyone who has lived in St. Louis County for any length of time can remember the landmark "Sign of the Dove" at West County Center.

DES PERES However, remembering specific stories or details about the "dove" could make you famous.

The 83-foot-high image migrated into storage in July while the center, which was constructed in 1969, underwent a redevelopment project. The center is set to reopen Sept. 20, along with a new and modernized dove.

As part of the grand opening for the center, local author Lynne Lang is compiling stories and photos of the dove to be published in her book, "Under the Dove, a Collection of Memories."

The idea for the book started after the dove was removed last summer from its perch atop the center's parking lot at Manchester Road and Interstate 270 in Des Peres.

"I moved to St. Louis in the mid-'60s and I remember the mall being built. We all used to meet under the dove," Lang said.

Every time Lang and her friends passed by the spot where the dove once hovered, she would say someone should do something on the history and memories of the dove.

"They would say, 'Then why don't you?'," Lang said.

She then contacted Sean Phillips, Westfield Shoppingtown's group marketing coordinator for the Midwest region, and told him about her idea. Westfield owns West County Center.

"We began working as a partnership," she said.

Lang now is looking for individuals to submit memories. Anyone with stories, photographs, drawings, memorabilia or trivia may contribute to the book, she said.

The $232 million redevelopment project will double the size of the center to about 1.2 million square feet, Phillips said.

The center had been 584,000 square foot and featured a food court, Famous-Barr and J.C. Penney department stores, as well as about 60 specialty stores. The redeveloped center will feature a new Famous-Barr — which opened last year — a renovated J.C. Penney, a larger food court and about 170 specialty stores.

When completed, the new center also will include two other department stores — the only Nordstrom's store in Missouri and a Lord & Taylor store.

Submissions for the book are due by April 15. Those interested may obtain more information about submitting memorabilia by visiting the web site at www.underthedove.com.

Westfield helped to gather stories for this book by publicizing it.
Courtesy West Suburban Journals, Jennifer Pope, Staff writer

The subplots within the book project were a surprise to me also. The absolute joy in meeting the many men and women who helped me write the history of the Dove added yet another dimension to my experience. I discovered that these individuals had such character! Like myself, each had a story to tell that had a professional and a personal side. As they worked to preserve and protect the Dove, they also dealt with personal challenges – births, deaths, illnesses, marriages, and divorces. Their interviews gave me a deep appreciation for not only their hard work, but also for them as individuals. For all these men and women, I am very grateful.

The memories and striking experiences people shared connect the Dove to a deeper level of the human spirit. When I collected the stories each week, I prepared to discover anything from a short humorous poem to a detailed narrative of a funny, sad, or even tragic memory. As you read this book, perhaps you will experience the same range of emotion that I did while writing it. I hope you connect to the deeper meaning in each contributor's story and their belief in the importance of sharing that story with readers.

Each unique story shares one common link – the gentle, white symbol that today is gracefully poised more than 80 feet high up into the air. Many phone calls received during construction of Westfield Shoppingtown West County came from individuals concerned that the Dove would never return. Some simply wanted to share their sentiments about it. The Dove has indeed returned to its perch and is here to stay. This book is intended to recognize all those individuals who worked to preserve this timeless landmark and those who treasure it.

Lynne Lang

Acknowledgments

"Mom, it's like you always say, 'If you can do this you can do anything!' Congratulations – you did it!"
Audrey Lang

A positive attitude is the best companion on any journey, and this book project is no exception. For me, fervent prayer and encouragement from many wonderful people fuel that attitude. My husband kept telling me that I was "unstoppable," which helped to build momentum for writing the book. Thanks, Gary, for tolerating my "bird brain" for these past months as I have indeed been "unstoppable" in talking about the West County Bird!

My children motivated my efforts with their constant encouragement and support. Each one has a unique way of offering a cheerful presence and demonstrating extraordinary strength when the need arises. They echo back those inspiring statements I have lavished on them over the years. Thanks for listening, even when you didn't look like you were!

I have this awesome group of former co-workers, the Fans, who have inspired me immeasurably over the past four years during our get-togethers. Thanks for helping even out the ups and downs of life. We've had the greatest conversations over many artipeggio pizzas and our laughter has given me the best fuel I could ever ask for. "Fan" Connie, you and Arlo were amazing at bringing "all hands on deck." I thought you were just coming over to read the material as I was writing! Good friend, Gary Whitlock, I hope this won't be our last project together. Thanks!

Diana Wilhold has been a wonderful manager at BJC HealthCare, helping me to manage my work schedule while completing this book. Over the past four years as a school health educator, she has given me the freedom to create meaningful health programs for students, teachers, and parents. Thanks for allowing so many wonderful ideas to develop from the limitless possibilities of what we can do to keep kids healthy. That has contributed to my belief in my ability to write this book.

My BJC co-workers encouraged and inspired me both personally and professionally. Thanks for making our work environment such a positive place to work and play! Thanks, too, to Donna Dalessandro – for your "bird's eye view." You've been a good creative partner during the journey!

With all these terrific people around me, I was able to step out confidently to tackle this writing task. Sean Phillips, Associate Regional Marketing Director for Westfield, was my first contact. He immediately liked the idea of writing a book and his assistance has been invaluable. He offered Priscilla Visintine's assistance with media and provided contacts with current and former Westfield and May Company employees.

Interviewing became a leg of the journey that offered inspiration all its own. Thanks to Joe Thaler for the contributions galore, to Helen Weiss for her history, to Dean Percival for materials contributed during my grand tour of General Sign Company. Dean, you definitely live up to the nickname "walking encyclopedia." I appreciate the awesome picture and historical information from Bill Trucksess and the history, contacts, materials, and great photographs from Rick Lahr and Doug Harms. Thanks for your phone call, Pam Wingbermuehle, and a special thanks to Jennifer Petrowsky for helping with history and the great collection of photos and ads. Also, Jim Mohrmann was very willing to allow me to hang around the shop at Signcrafters, Inc.

Former mayors Sharon Burkhardt and Jody Griggs, you were very gracious to accept the phone calls and open up your kitchens to me! Thanks also to Pep Tomasovic for the loan of *A History of Des Peres, Missouri.* It certainly made the history chapter easier to write.

Without Karen Berger and her wonderful staff this book would not have been published. Thanks, Karen, for taking this bird book "under your wing" – I cannot begin to tell you how much I appreciate what you've done for me. Thanks to Caroline Reich for helping with the details I could not have done myself. Thank you also to Carolita Deter and Diane Beasley for making this finished book possible.

The inspiration for the book led me to many wonderful contributors who shared their stories. You contributed the biggest part of the book. Thank you for the legacy you are now a part of and thank you for your many encouraging words. Many days I would open my mail and read a story that had a personal message about how you liked the idea of the book or you were sure it would be a best seller. These small gestures were good reminders of how important attitude is, because they inspired me to work just an hour or two longer before turning the lights out at night.

Finally, a special thanks to all those who find this book interesting enough to take home and treasure. It is a great collection of remembrances, history, and stories. I hope you enjoy reading it as much as I enjoyed preparing it.

This book has been a unique writing experience. For many years, my constant reminder to myself has been, "If I can do this, I can do anything!" This expression has inspired me to set and achieve many goals, both big and small. When I reflected on the power of that simple statement I realized that it needed to be passed on to my children as good advice. I hope it inspires them, too.

I persevere in faith, giving thanks to God in all things

Contents

Chapter 1

WORD ON THE BIRD FROM LOCAL PERSONALITIES

The Dove is essential to the history of Des Peres. It symbolizes the civic pride that comes from within this community. We are committed to preserving that tradition through our partnership with the City of Des Peres, and we share that pride.

Sean Phillips
Associate Regional Marketing
Director, Westfield Corporation

During the years after West County Center opened, many callers expressed their sentiment for the Dove. It seemed surprising that the public took to this icon so quickly. The local media was eager to cover stories of West County activities. The Dove became the identifier in advertisements by incorporating such phrases as, "West County Center, at the sign of the Dove."

The Dove has been a symbol of pride for many St. Louisans. A few local personalities took time to share special sentiments which are contained in this chapter.

FAMOUS·BARR
A DIVISION OF THE MAY DEPARTMENT STORES COMPANY

DUANE T. NICKS
CHAIRMAN

(314) 444-2731
FAX (314) 444-2743

Dear Readers,

When Famous-Barr and The May Department Stores Company introduced the Dove to West County Center in 1969, all of St. Louis claimed it as a landmark. Since then, it has remained an important part of the landscape at Westfield Shoppingtown West County.

Famous-Barr has a proud tradition of serving St. Louis with exceptional retail stores, and the West County store has been a part of that history. At its opening, the community took great pride in celebrating West County Center as one of its newest and most exciting malls. That pride has inspired many dedicated people to preserve the Dove as a great symbol even today as the new Westfield Shoppingtown West County reopens. This book is rich in revealing the history and memories of those individuals.

Famous-Barr is honored to be part of this commemorative book, and celebrates the Dove as it returns to the West County skyline.

Sincerely,

City of Des Peres
Missouri

Rick Lahr
Mayor
E-Mail: dpmayor@mvp.net

Doug Harms
City Administrator

Aldermen

Ward One
Kathleen Gmelich
John Parker

Ward Two
Jim Kleinschmidt
Paul Raczkiewicz

Ward Three
Jim Doering
Paul Fingerhut

Dear Readers:

The West County Dove has been perched high above Interstate 270 at West County Center in the City of Des Peres for nearly 34 years. Over time it has become a landmark feature and a symbol for both the shopping center and the city itself.

As a lifelong resident of Des Peres, I don't remember life without "the Dove." It is a symbol and reminder of my youth. I cannot count the number of times that we used it as a meeting place for friends. "We'll meet under the Dove" was heard almost as frequently as references to gathering at the Parkmoor. It was also a landmark to tell travelers how to get to Des Peres. "When you see the Dove, you are almost there…." The Dove is a part of the landscape of Des Peres that city officials wanted to preserve in the redevelopment and preservation of Westfield Shoppingtown West County as a regional shopping center.

The initial reaction of the "Californians" (Westfield's headquarters) to the concept of incorporating the Dove into the "new West County Center" was disbelief and skepticism. Surely we were joking and would eventually allow them to create a new, more vibrant and modern logo for the shopping center. Eventually, they saw the wisdom of preserving the landmark, which is as well known to native St. Louis Countians as the Arch might be to tourists visiting St. Louis. You just knew you were in Des Peres when you saw "the Dove."

As Westfield studied redevelopment concepts and marketing research for the new center, they too began to appreciate the landmark significance of the Dove as a regional symbol for Des Peres and of Westfield Shoppingtown West County. Not only have they agreed to retain the symbol, but they have chosen to refurbish the old Dove and bring it back as a focal point along the Interstate 270 landscape atop a new pole sign.

How strongly did city officials feel about incorporating the Dove in the Westfield Shoppingtown? The city tried to negotiate retaining the Dove in the redevelopment agreement. We were successful in requiring that preservation of the Dove be part of zoning approvals for the new shopping center as a part of an overall approval of the sign package.

How important was the symbol of the Dove to the community? You only had to see the size of the crowd and their reactions when the Dove was turned off in February 2001 to allow for its removal and storage during construction. A large crowd of residents gathered, each with a different story about some memory of an event that revolved around meeting "under the Dove."

Rick Lahr
Mayor – City of Des Peres

12325 Manchester Road • Des Peres, Missouri 63131 • Phone (314) 966-4600 • Fax (314) 966-2607
Relay Missouri: 1-800-735-2966 TDD

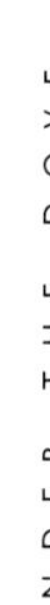

For many years, the Dove at West County Center represented the place to shop for quality. West County was far more than a regional shopping center. It had become Midtown for a fast-growing region. With the development of Highway 270, it was minutes away from three major highway intersections. We used to gather "under the Dove" and go on to other points before or after we shopped.

Today, with the St. Louis County region aging and in danger of becoming stagnant, this new face-lift with the Nordstrom anchor will breathe new life into our region. It will be a beautiful answer to urban sprawl. "Attract them to stay rather than fence them in!"

Anita Yeckel
State Senator, District 1

Having lived in Des Peres for twenty years, it seems I have seen the Dove a million times. As a symbol of peace and love, it always gives me a feeling of comfort. I'm glad it's remaining.

Buzz Westfall
St. Louis County Executive

West County Center was rather off my South Side turf, but it had one of the prettiest shopping center signs I'd ever seen. And it was just like West County to give us the Bird.

Elaine Viets
Mystery Writer

The Dove is like Stan the Man. When you got to Busch Stadium to see the Cardinals and you were meeting someone there, you always met at the Stan the Man statue outside the stadium. "Meet you at Stan…" was the phrase. Stan is central, visible, and easy to get to, and everybody knows where it is. The Dove is the same type of symbol. If you have friends or family coming from out of town, you give them directions to "meet under the Dove."

The St. Louis area Boy Scouts have a trip that they take to New Mexico to backpack and it includes scouts from all over the metro area. The trip leaves from the Dove.

Glenn Zimmerman
WEATHER DEPARTMENT, KTVI FOX 2

> **Bird Bit**
>
> *What's the word on the Bird? How big is it anyway?*
>
> •
>
> The dimensions of the Bird: 24 feet long and 20 feet tall

. . . .

I live in West County, and always found something slightly reassuring about seeing the Dove as I drove to the mall or other places. For some strange reason I have missed it while it's been gone! It's a real landmark in West County, and things just won't be right with the world until it's flying high again.

Nan Wyatt, Co-host
TOTAL INFORMATION AM

. . . .

One memory I have dates back to 1948, when I drove my girlfriend to the Manchester Drive-In Theatre. With the top up, my 1923 Model T (Touring Model) stood seven or eight feet high, so as you can imagine, the people behind us could not see the screen. I can't even remember what movie was showing, but

Ted Drewes Frozen Custard is another local landmark.
Courtesy Ted Drewes

people started honking at us! Finally we decided to move over to the end of the row of parked cars so mine didn't block their view.

That girl eventually became my wife, and now we live in West County near that spot where the old drive-in used to be – which today is a shopping mall. West County Center became her favorite place to shop, and we are looking forward to shopping at the new Westfield Shoppingtown. The West County Dove has been a part of the history of Des Peres, and just like Ted Drewes Frozen Custard, it seems as though it has always been there!

A landmark is tough to preserve. Landmarks give us a sense of the history of an area, or a building, because of the memories we can share. I didn't realize that Ted Drewes was a landmark until people started telling me it was, and then when we celebrated our 50th Anniversary in 1981, it was a great party! I hope the Dove will be around to celebrate 50 years and beyond.

Ted Drewes
OWNER, TED DREWES FROZEN CUSTARD

When you tell people from out of town, "I'm from St. Louis," the response is usually "Oh yeah, the city with the Arch" or "the home of Budweiser." But when was the last time you visited either? That's not to say we don't appreciate our landmark favorites, but for St. Louisians they just exist; pillars in our landscape with no significant impact on our daily routine.

When you talk about landmarks that truly play a role in our lives, few loom larger than that Bird in the sky. It's as common to St. Louisans as the high school we attended. It's like the zoo; everyone knows how to get there. Like the Mississippi, it marks a geographical direction. The river is east, the Dove is west. It shines over

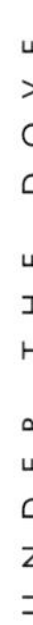

Interstate 270 like a lighthouse beacon. Strangers to our city would never pay a visit to the "Bird" that we know so well. It's not exactly art. It's not an architectural wonder. It's not the wings of Lindbergh. It doesn't give away free samples of beer. But perhaps that is why we cherish that white creature on a pole so much; it's distinctly ours. Not a national monument or a "King of Beers." Not a tourist trap. Not even a conversation piece. It's just a marquee marking a mall that everyone knows, everyone can find, and everyone takes for granted.

My car has been parked in the Dove's shadow on countless occasions. Road trips to play in baseball tournaments; we met at the mall. Car pools to Blues games; free parking under the Dove. Visiting friends and family who can't follow directions; we always met under the big white Bird just off 270.

I heard someone say once that the Dove should be out in front of a Church as a symbol of the Holy Spirit, not designating a destination of commercial capitalism. But I would argue that this Dove represents the "Spirit" of St. Louis. A common ground for all of us, no matter our age, race, or high school of origin. It did not discriminate between Fords and Cadillacs. American cars always parked alongside Beemers and Mercedes. Whether in a pickup or a Porsche, we all could meet and greet at the Dove. No membership required. No hassles from mall security. After all, if we could make it to the Dove to meet our friends, chances are we were paying customers at Christmas time.

When recent renovations brought the big Bird down, it left a weird void in my daily commute. It was my halfway marker to West Port. That beacon that shined through rain, snow, and fog.

I'm certainly glad that the folks at Westfield Shoppingtown West County will bring back our Bird when the construction is complete. Surely they recognize that some things are too traditional to discard. Some birds are just are meant to fly forever.

Dan Buck
HOST, SHOW ME ST. LOUIS AND THE KTRS MORNING SHOW

Mrs. Lawrence K. Roos was among those on hand to celebrate West County Center's grand opening 25 years ago. She and Sanford J. Zimmerman, president of Famous-Barr, cut a ribbon to free 125 homing pigeons.

Courtesy Suburban Journals West County, February 23, 1994 edition on 25th anniversary

I grew up in the Ballwin/Chesterfield area and for me, the sign of the Dove is definitely a landmark. As teenagers, my girlfriends and I would always meet at the Dove when we went shopping. Even though there were usually parking spaces closer to the door, we knew we couldn't miss each other if the Dove was our designated meeting place.

When my family would visit relatives in Memphis, we would come up Highway 55, then get on 270 to go home. Every time, just after we would pass Highway 44, the whole family would yell "It's the Dove sign – we're almost home!" and we would exit at Manchester Road to get home.

One more thing. . . the Dove has always reminded me of a Christmas ornament we had on our Christmas tree when I was young.

Wendy Wiese
550 KTRS Radio Personality

Chapter 2

History of the Dove

dove (duv) n. *1. Any of a smaller species of pigeon: often used as a symbol of peace. 2. An advocate of measures which avoid or end wars. (Webster's New World Dictionary, 1996.)*

The subject of this book, our beloved West County Dove, is a stylized version of a species of common doves. Doves belong to more than 300 species of pigeons, although pigeons are usually larger than doves. Two species that are most popular in aviaries and as pet birds are the ringneck (or Barbary) dove and the diamond dove *(Geopelia cuneata)*. The landmark Dove at West County has outlasted its live counterparts, whose lifespan is usually about 12 to 15 years. However, approximately every 15 years the Dove was removed for renovation.

Have you ever wondered why we have a dove overlooking a shopping center? What is the point? How did it get there? Who designed it? Answers to these and many other questions were discovered through interviews with the individuals who have preserved this important landmark. Recalling the Dove's story begins in the 1930's with the history of the land it is perched on in the City of Des Peres.

Doug Harms, the current City Administrator for Des Peres, provided contact information for reaching Jody Griggs, former Mayor of Des Peres (1970-1972). Jody and her fellow Des Peres resident, Pep Tomosovic, furnished a brief history of this suburb of St. Louis that began in the 1800's and was formally incorporated in 1934.

Shortly thereafter in 1940, the Manchester Drive-In Theatre was built at the site of Westfield Shoppingtown West County. This landmark theater, built on a 50-acre tract of land, was among the first of its kind in the St. Louis area. It operated for 27 years until the land was purchased to build West County Center in 1967.

In the early 1950's, Des Peres formed a Planning and Zoning Commission to oversee the rapid growth of homes and commercial businesses in the area. Recognizing the need for a more sophisticated form of government to regulate this growth, in 1954, residents voted in favor of the question, "Shall the Town of

Manchester Drive-In Theatre around 1950.
Courtesy City of Des Peres

Easter Sunday service at Manchester Drive-In around 1950.
Courtesy City of Des Peres

Des Peres become a City of the Fourth Class under the name and style the City of Des Peres?" This decision paved the way for a stronger local government, and the Chairman of the Board of Trustees was then elevated to Mayor of the City.

These changes were important during the rapid transition from a rural village to a bustling community with a few small retail shops and markets. Local sales tax approval resulted in funding for local government and services for residents, including street maintenance and public safety. Manchester Road had always been a hub of business activity. Now Des Peres was positioned to seek commercial businesses that would serve to enhance the community. Shopping malls were becoming a popular concept nationwide, and it was soon agreed that this was the only way to accommodate the growing number of consumers in Des Peres.

In 1965, Interstate 244 (now 270) was opened, and its exits onto Manchester expanded the possibilities for a new surge of commercial growth. The Manchester Drive-In Theatre was sold in 1967, and on February 1969, West County Center held its grand opening – complete with a Dove on the parking lot that overlooked Highway 270 and Manchester Road.

The grand opening of West County Center, February 20, 1969.
Courtesy City of Des Peres

In the summer of 1968, May Stores and Shopping Centers (a large part of May Company) moved a house trailer to the property at Manchester and 270. I worked for them as a carpenter.

A drive-in theater that occupied the property was being torn down and some grading was being done for the new shopping center. I gutted the house trailer and made it a field office. The office was to be used for plans and material needed by Mr. Norm Barth, Superintendent of Construction. Mr. Barth was the man who kept an eye on any work done by the contractors and subcontractors on behalf of May Company.

After the center was completed, May Stores and Shopping Centers maintained the center until May Company got out of the shopping center business. I put in many hours of maintenance and decoration for holidays.

Harold B. Sykora, Local 5
CARPENTER FOR MAY COMPANY

Aerial view of the new West County Center.
Courtesy City of Des Peres

Thomas Christenson raised the pigeons that were released to mark the grand opening of the new West County Center.
Courtesy Margaret Hoeft

I'm excited about the return of the Dove because my father had a part in the installation and maintenance.

My parents, Thomas A. and Oma N. Christenson, lived in Overland, Missouri. They owned a good-sized lot on what used to be the old streetcar line, which later turned into the widened four-lane Midland Avenue. My father emigrated from Denmark, where he raised pigeons. When my father and mother purchased the house and land on Midland, he built a pigeon house and became active in the local pigeon racing clubs.

Somehow the media thought it would be a good idea for my father to take a crate of his birds and release them under the Dove. He was interviewed by John Auble, and

his picture appeared in the Post-Dispatch (or was it the Globe Democrat?). After the release of the birds, my father invited Mr. Auble back to our home, where they had quite a visit.

My mom and dad are no longer with us, but I'm sure that was one of the proudest moments of dad's life.

Margaret Hoeft

I remember passing by West County Center on opening day as the doves were released and watching as they flew away.

I also met my friend Clarice under the Dove as we got together to celebrate birthdays or just planned a visit. She was a proof reader and I was a typesetter. Clarice drove a big old Lincoln Continental from her home in Belleville, Illinois. I lived in Hazelwood, so the Dove was a good halfway point to meet.

The Dove was a wonderful and visible place to meet. Meeting under the Dove was a great start to wonderful times we had together.

Mary Bailey

The young Joe Thaler, designer of the original Dove as part of the signage for West County Center in 1969.
Courtesy Joe Thaler

Joe Thaler, who designed the Dove, was born and raised in Erie, Pennsylvania. He began his art and graphic training at Erie Technical High School and continued at the Columbus College of Art and Design in Columbus, Ohio. In 1966, he moved to St. Louis and began working as an illustrator for Famous-Barr and May Stores, Inc. Thaler later began to freelance with Center Promotions, a new agency that worked with May Stores throughout the country. In 1976, he left to take a position at Gardner Advertising, until Greenville, South Carolina, became his home in 1981. There he worked for Henderson Advertising and in 1990, decided to open his own graphic design studio. Today he does business as Joe, the Creative Guy. Thaler enjoys offering expertise in graphics and advertising, and hopes that more of his work will endure the test of time as the Dove has. Here is what Thaler reveals about his landmark of local fame:

"May Stores were beginning to implement a very aggressive growth strategy with West County Center in the relatively unspoiled high-dollar west suburbs of town. As difficult as it is to believe today, little existed in that area of Manchester Road and the newly opened Highway 270. Carefully planned and often restricted residential neighborhoods were quick to demand a service industry that could satisfy the growing community.

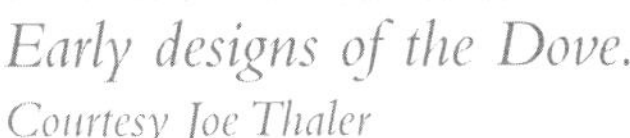

Early designs of the Dove.
Courtesy Joe Thaler

"West County Center offered a theme that seemed to fit the community. Planners selected a European village to be the model for the architectural theme. The mass would showcase a lovely central fountain and all the store facades would replicate shops and boutiques found in charming European towns. But what of signage? What kind of location markings would be appropriate for such an area? That's where I came in.

"The May Stores management team with whom I was working, asked me to contribute designs for signs, logos, or whatever else I thought would be right for this venture. I instantly saw it as a challenge.

"The year was 1968, and the Vietnam War was still on everyone's mind. A restless generation of youth struggled with the capitalism and worldly progress of their parents. Musical artists such as Janice Joplin, Bob Dylan, and Joan Baez filled the airwaves with sentiment about this conflict. Joni Mitchell's song, 'Big Yellow Taxi,' echoed '...they paved paradise and put up a parking lot.' This further deepened a sense of eco-consciousness about what was happening to our world.

"Strangely, at the age of 28, I found myself with one foot in each camp: Save nature and the planet, and do my job with a commercial developer. The idealist in me said I could do both! Early in the design process, I relied on past experience with signage and put any logo symbols and/or words into contained shapes. After all, this was the way signage was done. But in time I realized that nothing traditional felt right, and I began to go beyond what was considered traditional. Even management seemed to be open to something different and encouraged broader thinking. I didn't want to replace paradise with crass parking lot aesthetics!

"By now I was convinced that a symbol would offer the best solution. After rejecting such thoughts as lions, dragons, and the floriculture commonly used in European design, I began to contemplate the graceful, nonthreatening, and even calming effect of birds. I thought of the scenes of French fountains surrounded by people whose only friends were the park birds. I even considered the eagle, but dismissed it because it could be perceived as too aggressive. Given the war climate, the eagle seemed too symbolic of the military.

"My designs began to take shape as simple, unidentifiable birds with outstretched wings that soared peacefully over the land. Some birds were integrated into the confines of signage shapes, but eventually I envisioned a three-dimensional sculptured bird on a pole.

Joe Thaler today, poised on his motorcycle. He resides in South Carolina, and is self-employed as Joe, the Creative Guy.
Courtesy Joe Thaler

Early designs of the Dove.
Courtesy Joe Thaler

"I was certain that this symbol needed no words. If done right and placed strategically high overhead, it would be strong enough as a mark to stand alone as a location identifier. To my surprise, those in authority agreed! We decided that signs including the words 'West County Center' would be placed low to the ground, and only at entrances. I can't tell you how happy and thankful I was to have been working with what I felt were very progressive, forward-thinking developers.

"After the final approval, the bird design was sent off to sign builders and erected at West County Center. I didn't really think about what kind of bird it was. Even during development some called it a dove. So be it. Doves were a symbol of peace and good will. Not a bad statement for the sixties.

"To help 'seed' the white bird as a symbol for the center, advertising illustrations featured flocks of birds around a fountain to enhance the Euro village look. Whenever appropriate the white birds were integrated into ad designs.

"Although I had hoped to end up with a symbol constructed a bit more dimensionally, I was still proud of the initiative taken by May Stores and for their final selection that ultimately became known as 'the Dove.' I'm also fascinated when I hear a tale involving the Dove or a mention of it in the news. It rekindles my own remembrances of using it as a measure of where I was as I traveled: 'Almost to the hockey rink in Creve Coeur' or 'halfway to the airport' and 'Ah, Manchester Road at West County Center.' "

2 D—COMMUNITY PRESS—Wed., Feb. 19, 1969

WHITE DOVE IS CENTER SYMBOL

The Community Press was on hand for the "topping out" ceremony of the sign raising at the new West County Center. The sign, depicting a white dove, official symbol of the new center, was built in Philadelphia, Pa., but erected on the west county site adjacent to Interstate 244 by the Simon Sign Erection Company, of St. Louis. The size of the logo can be determined by comparison with a workman, below, alongside the wing section of the 2-piece unit.

The Dove installation for grand opening, February 20, 1969.
Courtesy Famous-Barr

When Thaler completed his design, it was submitted to several companies, but he did not have information on the company that produced the finished product. A story submitted by Pat Rush states, "My Uncle Alvin Kampen drew and designed the Dove sign." He was general manager for Federal Sign and Signal at the time, however documentation is no longer available. His wife, Lucille, claims that their grandchildren refer to the Dove as "Grandpa's Sign."

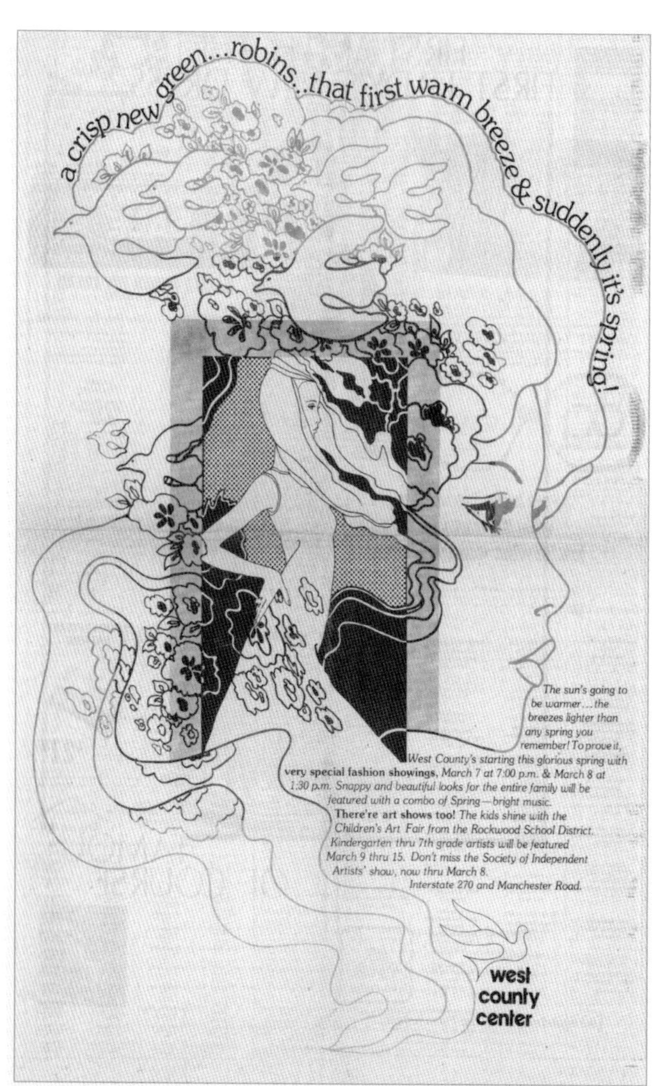

Advertisements from the early 1970's.
Courtesy Joe Thaler.

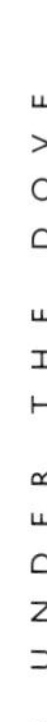

JULY SALE
AND SUMMER CLEARANCE
WEDNESDAY THRU SATURDAY JULY 7-10
west county center
Interstate 270 and Manchester Rd.

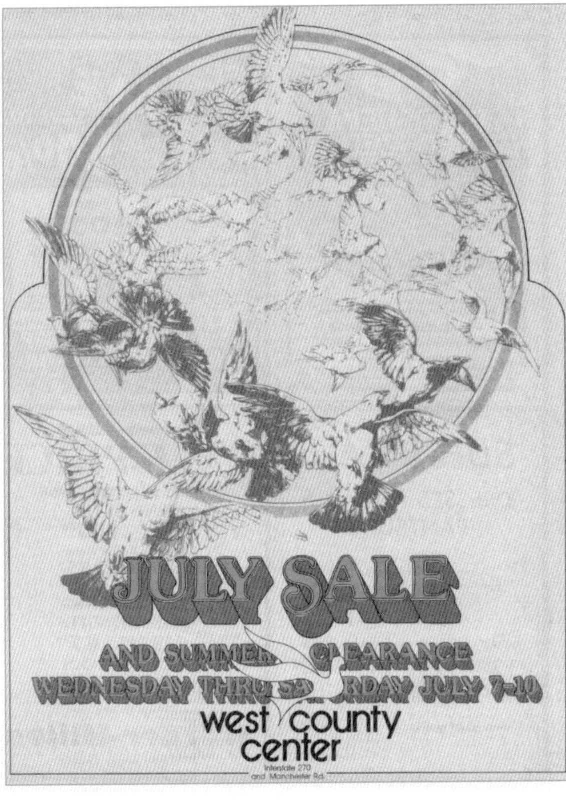

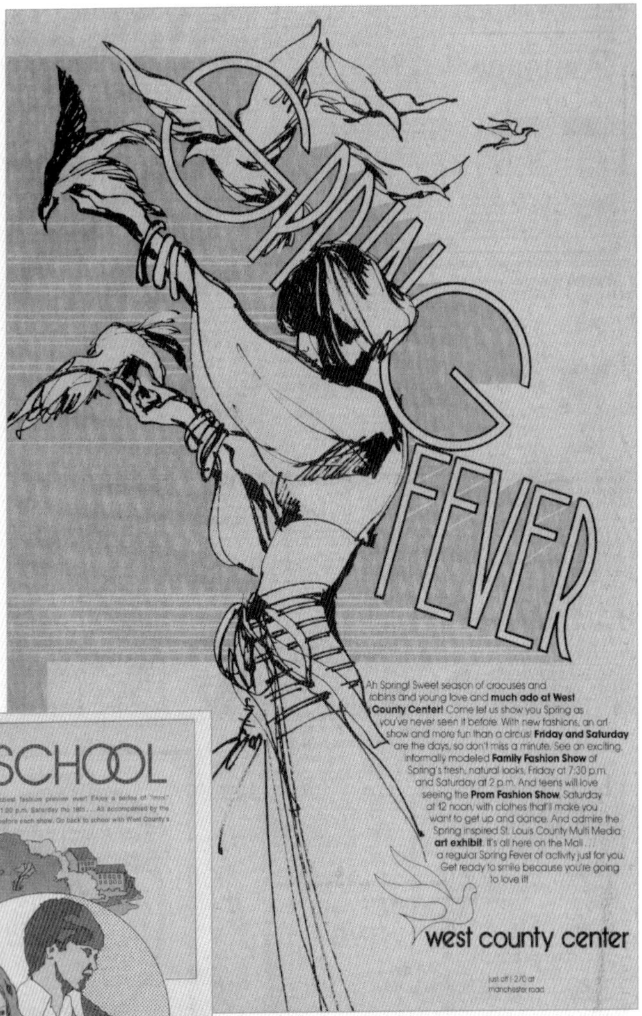
SPRING FEVER
Ah Spring! Sweet season of crocuses and robins and young love and **much ado at West County Center!** Come let us show you Spring as you've never seen it before. With new fashions, an art show and more fun than a circus! **Friday and Saturday** are the days, so don't miss a minute. See an exciting, informally modeled **Family Fashion Show** of Spring's fresh, natural looks, Friday at 7:30 p.m. and Saturday at 2 p.m. And teens will love seeing the **Prom Fashion Show**, Saturday at 12 noon, with clothes that'll make you want to get up and dance. And admire the Spring inspired St. Louis County Multi Media **art exhibit**. It's all here on the Mall . . . a regular Spring Fever of activity just for you. Get ready to smile because you're going to love it!
west county center
just off I-270 at manchester road

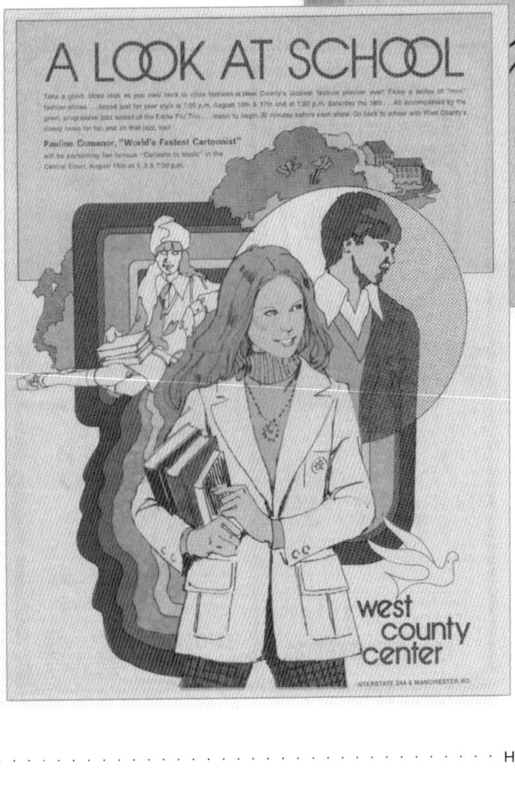
A LOOK AT SCHOOL
Pauline Comanor, "World's Fastest Cartoonist"
west county center

How tall is the original Dove?

•

In 1969, the height of the mounted Bird was 64 feet.

Helen Weiss, Divisional Vice President of Public Relations with Famous-Barr, provided an old newspaper article with vague details that directed the search for the manufacturer to Philadelphia Sign Company in New Jersey. This was a difficult piece of history to uncover, since many people involved in the early construction are no longer available for contact.

Bill Trucksess, President of Philadelphia Sign Company, mentioned that this was a very big job for what was then a small company in 1969. Since that time, his company has grown larger and has done many signs for May Company Stores, Inc. throughout the country. Little did he know at that time how this landmark would take its place in the history of Des Peres.

Enclosed are the photographs and our original order. At the top of the order it says Dimensional Graphics, Inc. This was a wholly owned subsidiary of Philadelphia Sign Company for accounting purposes.

As you can see, the total pylon price was $19,480, which in today's dollars would be $102,000. This was the first of a series of shopping centers for the May Company, for which we supplied signage.

A. William (Bill) Trucksess
PRESIDENT, PHILADELPHIA SIGN COMPANY

Area Code 609 829-1460

ORIGINAL ORDER FORM

No. 1970

DIMENSIONAL GRAPHICS, INC
7_ W. SPRING GARDEN STREET
PALMYRA, NEW JERSEY 08065

TYPED: 10/30/68

Order No. vbl Mr. Dwyer (order to follow) Dept. Date 19

Name THE MAY STORES SHOPPING CENTERS, INC.

Address 1541 Railway Express Building City St. Louis, Missouri

Ship To WEST COUNTY CENTER

Address ST. LOUIS, MO. City

WHEN SHIP	HOW SHIP	TERMS	BUYER	SALESMAN
Feb. 3, 1969 (Center opens approx. Feb. 20, 1969)				Harwitz (\$1,490.00)

1) One double faced pylon sign, fabricated as a free-form bird, per drawing #368-121. Overall size to be 20' high by 25' wide.

Face of the sign to be fabricated of 1/4" thick white Plexiglas. Casing and retaining angles to be galvannealed metal with a black, semi-matte, baked enamel finish.

Illumination to be 2 banks of 18 MM white cold cathode tubing, powered by 120 M.A. transformers. Tubing to be approximately 5" on center, spaced evenly over the entire face of the bird. There are to be no hot spots or shadows.

Structural support for the bird to be double angle iron yokes, supported by central pipe supports. (Sign.... \$17,000.00 (Footing... 1,300.00

Pole and footings to be as per drawing. Bottom of the bird to be 60' from grade. \$18,300.00

2) ~~Two~~ 3 pylon signs, per drawing #368-120. Diamonds to be 11'8" long by 6'9" high, overall. Face of the diamond to be one piece of 1/4" thick clear acrylic, decorated on the inside surface with black background and white bird and letters. Casing of the diamond to be galvannealed metal with black baked enamel finish. 2 @\$1,800.00 .... \$ 3,600.00
Footing @\$200.00 ... 400.00

Diamond to be internally illuminated by multiple rows of T-12 high output lamps. \$ 4,000.00

Structural support and footing, as per drawing.

NOTE: An alternate design for these two signs is being submitted to May Department Stores, showing an oval. Hold until decision is made.

Permits are to be obtained.

-CONT'D ON OTHER SIDE- D. G. ORDER #1970

Original work order, 1968.
Courtesy Philadelphia Sign Company

Courtesy Philadelphia Sign Company

I was a member of the Planning and Zoning Board of Des Peres when the May Company made application to build the West County Shopping Center in the 1960's. The architects appeared before the board to submit plans for review.

The initial and subsequent sets of drawings were submitted for review by our board. Each one of these plans included the infamous Dove sign as part of the project. So the board has known the Dove since we were in the early stages of planning and developing the mall.

To our surprise, when the final plans were submitted for approval to begin construction, the Dove had "flown off" the plans and in its place was a very large vertical sign showing May Company Shopping Center. This sign switch almost ended negotiations!

The board insisted on having the Dove back. The architect, along with May Company, threatened to scrap the entire project if we did not agree to the commercial sign. After much deliberation, a few of the board members persuaded the rest of the board to stick to our position. We insisted that the Dove should return.

Soon thereafter, we were presented with a new set of construction plans for approval – and the Dove returned to roost. The project was then completed to our satisfaction.

I would like to think that we were correct in our position, because the Dove has come to be a landmark and a symbol of good taste that represents the wholesome community of Des Peres. People from all over have met under the Dove to gather before traveling locally and throughout the state.

Wes Neu

Bird Bit

In order to install the Dove, how deep will workers need to dig?

•

a. 11 feet

b. 33 feet

c. 17 feet

•

Workers dug 17 feet deep in order to properly install the Dove. However, in 2002 when planning to install the new Dove, workers discovered an underground junction box. This simple 3-foot square box created some challenges for installers!

Installation of the Dove was a job for Simon Sign Erection Company. "Bill Simon, Sr. headed up that project in the late 60's," recalls his son, Bill. However, photographs and other documentation no longer exist. Bill Ryan also assisted in the installation.

Bill Ryan of Keller Sign Company maintained the Dove from 1969-1986. "It cost $75.00 per hour per man to maintain it – and that didn't include the cost of equipment," he noted.

He recalls, "The mall manager, Joe Masterson, would call me and say… 'It's out again.' Then I'd come out and climb up there - we actually could walk inside it. I'd say, 'Uncle Joe, that's a *big* Bird!'" Ryan also remembers having the task of repairing the Dove after a windstorm blew one side out.

The sign used cold cathode neon tubing (18 mm size), which was eventually replaced by fluorescent tubes. Ryan's son helped with the installation and maintenance. He remembers that his son was dating at the time and wrote, "Bill loves Sylvia" inside the sign on the metal framework before his son was married in 1972. In June of 2002, Bill and Sylvia celebrated 30 years of marriage.

Joseph Liberton (center) with his family. They called the Dove "Daddy's Bird."
Courtesy Dorothy (Cimaglia) Liberton

I'm sending this letter to you about the Bird at West County Shopping Center, because my husband, Joseph Liberton, was an electrician who wired it. We always called it "Daddy's Bird" when we passed it.

The day they first turned it on, we took all the kids to see it. Seven kids. After he died in 1984, we said Dad was watching us when we passed it. We would always say, "There is a little spot that he is sitting in watching us."

When they took it down I almost cried; it just wasn't the same without it. It meant a lot to us. Even our grandchildren asked what happened to Grandpa's Bird.

Dorothy (Cimaglia) Liberton

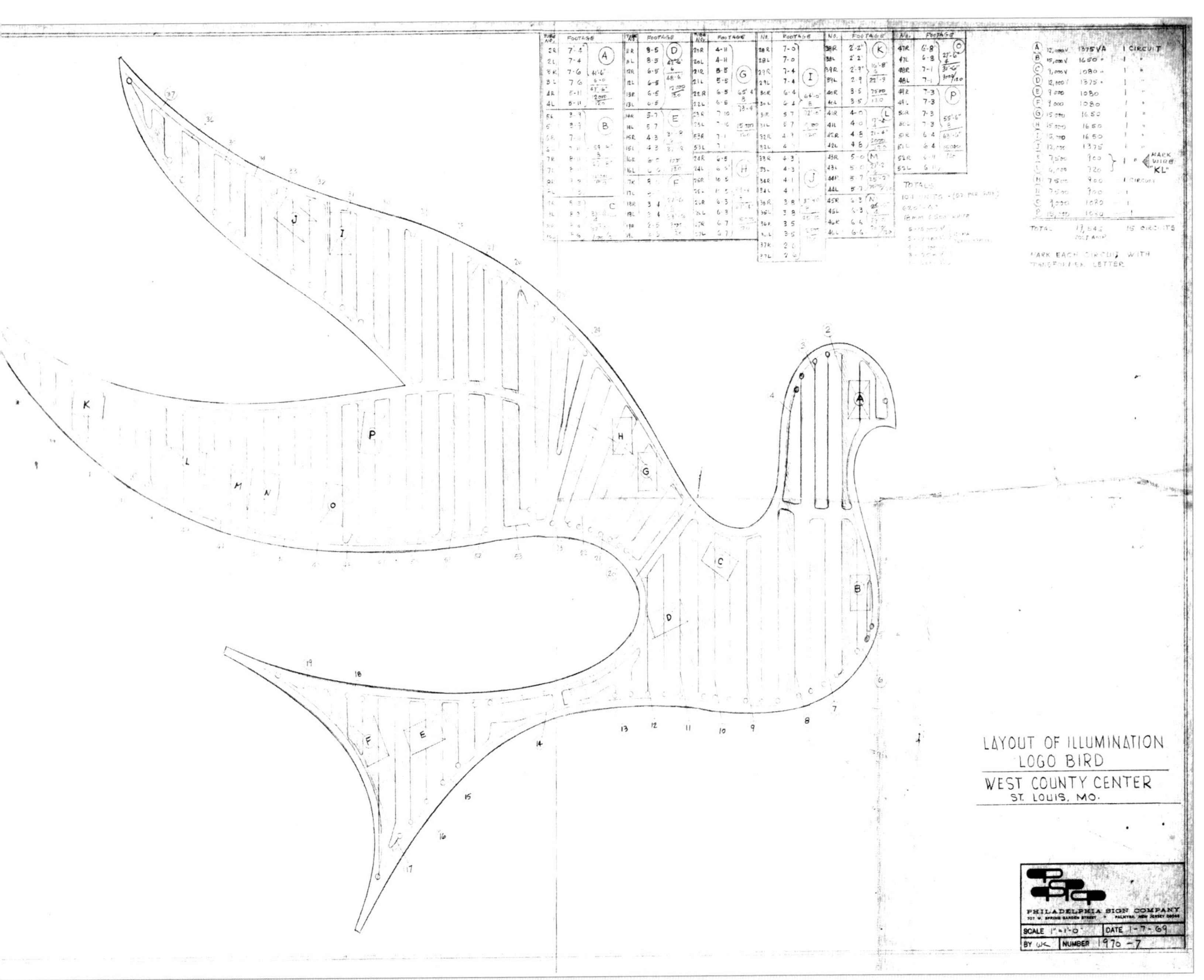

Layout of illumination, 1968.
Courtesy Bill and Marge Ryan

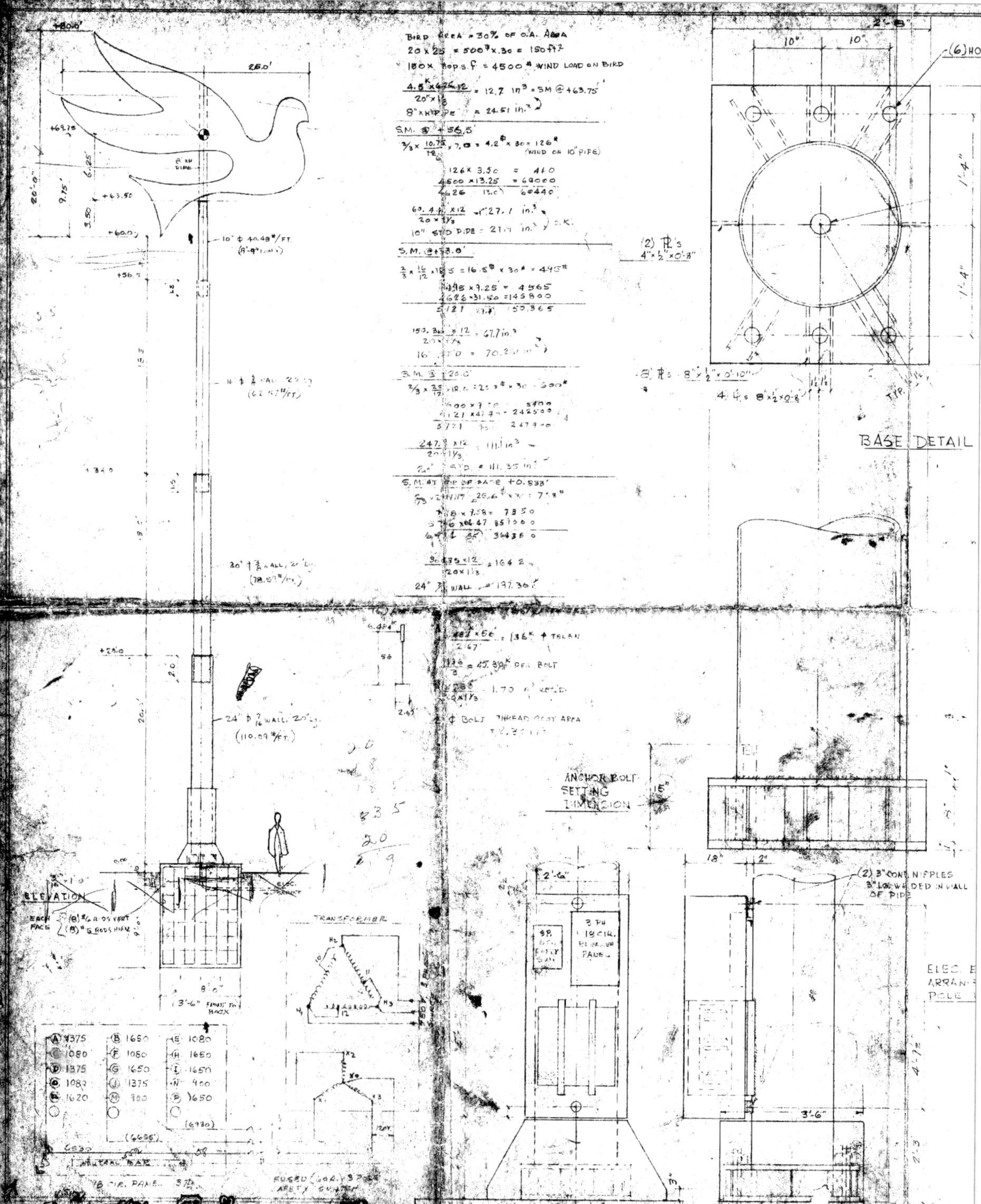

Original blueprint, 1968.

Courtesy Bill and Marge Ryan

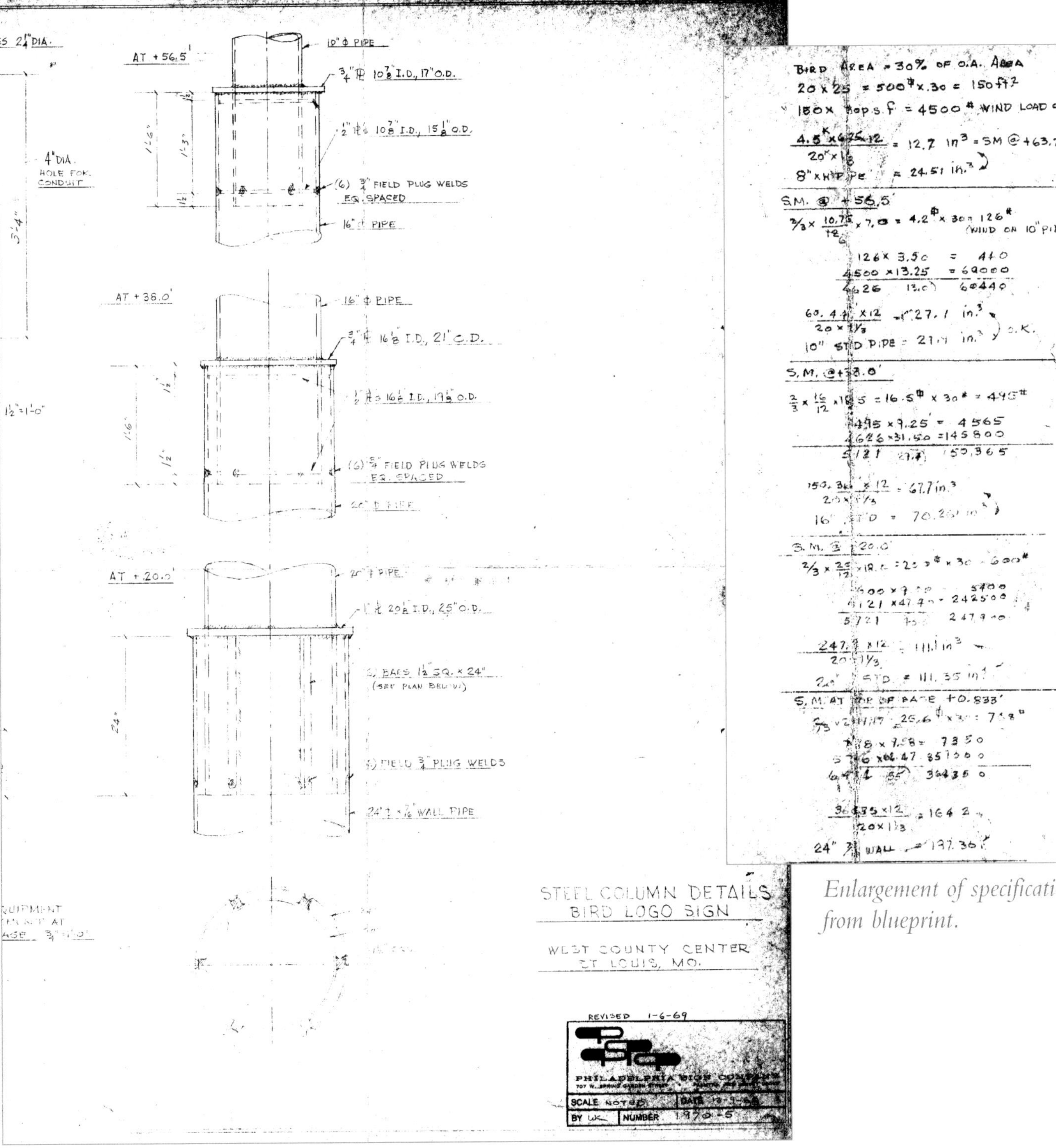

Enlargement of specifications from blueprint.

Chapter 3

WORKING UNDER THE SHADOW OF THE DOVE

I have enjoyed the Dove for many years. It is visible from my house, and I especially enjoy seeing it as a tree topper for the tree that is suspended below it each year at Christmas time.

Marion Pleis

Thousands of employees have worked at West County over the years. For some, it was an opportunity to earn extra spending money for holiday shopping. For others, it meant taking on a more important role as a manager or as an elected official for the local government of Des Peres. The information in this chapter offers readers a closer look at the Dove from the perspective of those who were in leadership positions within West County and the City of Des Peres.

Courtesy Westfield Shoppingtown West County and Jennifer Petrowsky

What was it like working in the shadow of a landmark of local fame? Pam (McLean) Wingbermuehle held the position of Marketing Director from 1982-87, producing brochures, ad campaigns, and other marketing projects for the center. By this time, the center was more than 15 years old and it was time for a face-lift. In 1986, Pam oversaw the renovation of the center – and the Dove. That following winter, a Christmas tree of lights became part of the Dove décor.

"Jerry Miller, manager at the time, had seen a tree of lights somewhere, and we decided to try it here," Pam said during an interview for the book. "We had Federal Sign Company come and measure the pole, then they made a steel structure with bolts to attach to it. It cost us around $18,000." Two-inch white bulbs were attached to the tree to light up the night during the holidays. Pam remembers, "Having the Dove as the top of the tree really was appealing as a visual symbol. People loved it."

During renovation of the center, the Dove was taken down for restoration. The theme for renovation featured Merlin the Sorcerer, touting the theme, "The Magic of West County – We're Changing Before Your Very Eyes!" A conservative Christian church nearby believed the mall Dove to be a Christian symbol. Members of the congregation expressed their outrage at its removal and possible replacement with a non-Christian symbol.

Courtesy Westfield Shoppingtown West County

What happened to the sign during the mall renovation? The Dove was removed and taken to General Sign Company in Cape Girardeau while Westfield was remodeling. At the time, Bill Rush was the salesman in St. Louis for General. He eagerly accepted the work order to update the lighting. The broken plastic faces and all the sheet metal were replaced. The work was completed under the direction of Pat Sulser and Dean Percival. Sulser did the drawing, and Percival worked with the shop in refurbishing the sign.

Bird Bit

Since 1969, what has it cost to light the Dove?

•

A. $56,000

•

B. $122,000

•

C. $72,000

•

D. $26,000

•

General Sign reports that based on a cost of eight cents per kilowatt-hour, since 1969, lighting the Dove has cost approximately $26,000.

"It was a big project," Percival recalled. "But that job really expanded the possibilities of what we could do, and since then we have done other larger jobs. One of those was a 40 foot square sign in Atlanta, Georgia, for Delta Airlines. We were a small company then, and today we have about 70 employees."

During the 1986 renovation, the thickness of the sign was increased by one foot. This enabled the metal cladding to accommodate the newer mercury vapor lighting. The sheet metal that holds the wiring and bulbs was once again finished in durable, acrylic, urethane paint, tinted "United Airlines Blue."

When the work was completed, the sign was brought back to West County once again. "The worst part of our sign business is getting the finished piece to the job site without damage," commented Rob Nicholas, sign installer for General. "It will never get that kind of jolting again." To transport the sign with minimal risk, it was shipped in two pieces, and metal support strips were bolted onto the wings. This also makes it possible to pass under wires and clear underpasses while en route to its destination.

The Dove was again taken down and placed in General's yard in February of 2001 while the old mall was being demolished. A tour of General's work area revealed new technology, such as computerized cutting machines and softer, thinner, and more durable plastics that can better withstand weather and time.

In June of 2002, however, the contract was awarded to Signcrafters, Inc., and the sign was moved to its new location to await the scheduled renovations. The new

CUSTOMER West County "DOVE" W. Co. Ctr. St. L. MO 63131 JOB NO. S-10060 DATE 6-16-86

DESCRIPTION ① D/F illum dove, approx 20'x24', same as old one, but 36" filler, merc. vapor illum. - per CC-494-S SALES PERSON Bill Rush

pg.____ of____

24'

20'

6½'

10'3"

Service doors as needed

re-use Stub pipe if poss.

116' perim.

ENG. BY PWS-DP

CONSTRUCTION

	QTY.	PART #	DESCRIPTION
563	500#	#7328	3/16 whiteplex faces - flat
450	250'	1½x1½x3/16"	S. ∠ double frame
315	350#	.063 A.	filler - 36" wide
108	120#	.063 A.	retainers - fabricated
1637			
520			12'-10" pipe
100			paint
2520 hrs. est.		7-01 DP	take down 7-9-01

ELECTRICAL ~~U.L. ☐~~ VOLTS 120

QTY.	PART #	DESCRIPTION	AMPS
21	175 W.	N. Am. Phillips MERCURY VAPOR LAMPS	
		(DELUXE WHITE)	
21	BALLAST	UNIV. # 1010-245 C-TC 175 W MERCURY VAPOR	1.7
21	LAMP	SOCKETS MOGUL	
21	HANDY	BOXES	

TOT. CIR. 2-25A. TOTAL AMPS 35.7

FINISH

DESCRIPTION	COLOR	NUMBER
CABINET & RET.	BLUE	42-233

A: ALUMINUM S: STEEL ∠: ANGLE SS: STAINLESS T.C.: TRIM CAP GEN. EED 12-84

Work order for General Sign to renovate the Dove in 1986.

Courtesy General Sign Company

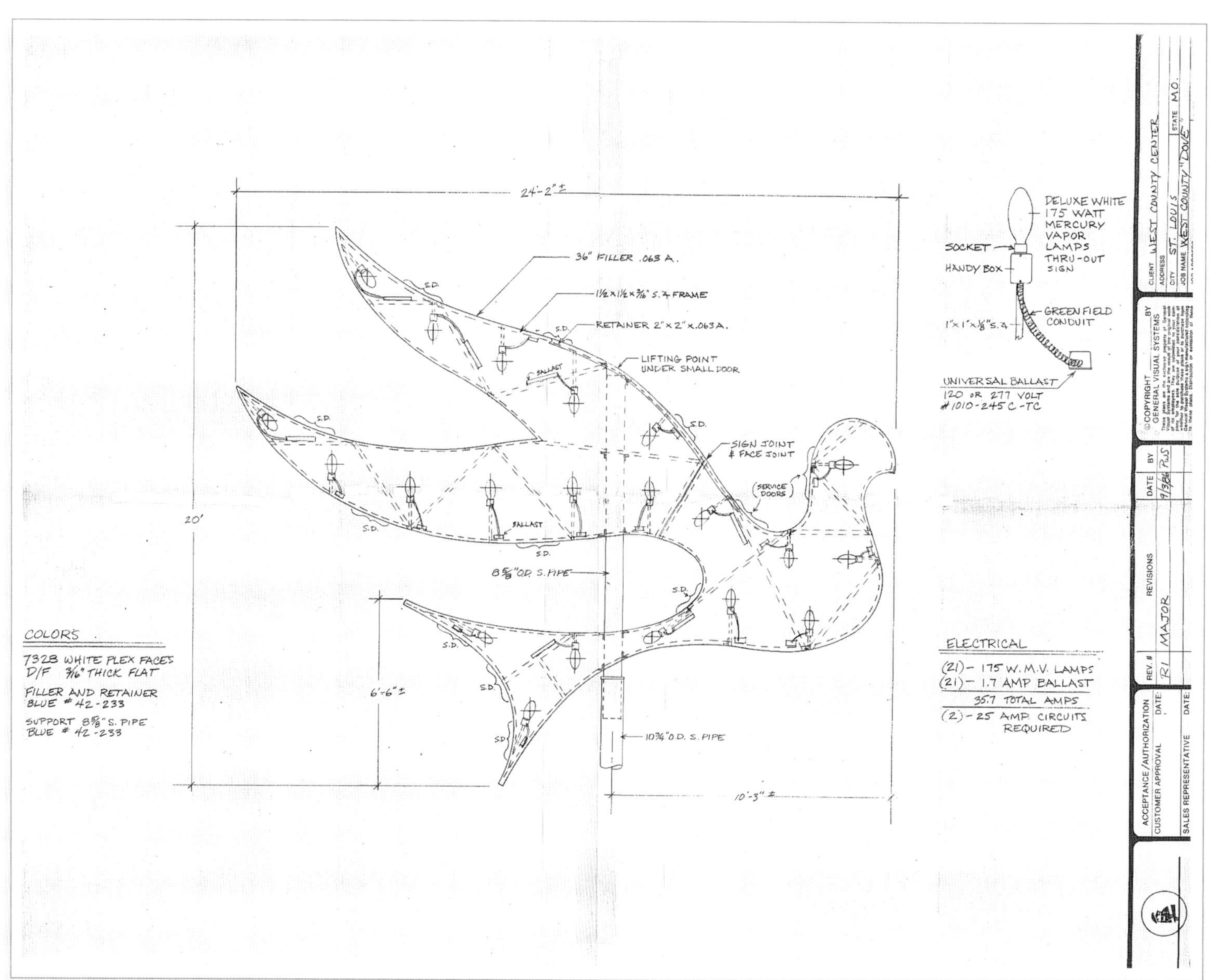

Working diagram for 1986 renovation.
Courtesy General Sign Company

will use mercury vapor lighting contained in a thinner, more flexible face, to allow the Dove to withstand the range of weather changes. West County signage was to be completed by Ultra Sign Company in California. However, Signcrafters was given the job of renovating the Dove, most likely because it was easier to keep the sign here in St. Louis.

Jim Mohrmann from Signcrafters noted that the renovated Dove will fly higher than ever at 83 feet once it is fastened to its telescopic pole. The aluminum casing on the newest bird will be painted with a two-part acrylic polyurethane, and the white face will be constructed using white lexan (3/16 mm thickness). Because the lexan comes in 10-foot rolls, the Dove will once again be done in two pieces. Moving the Dove to its spot in their shop was a difficult task due to the small signyard in the back of the shop on Washington Avenue in downtown St. Louis. "Dodging trees, cars, and fences was quite a challenge!" Mohrmann said.

The new Westfield awaits completion, and the return of the Dove to its home by the parking lot.
Photo by Nicholas Lang

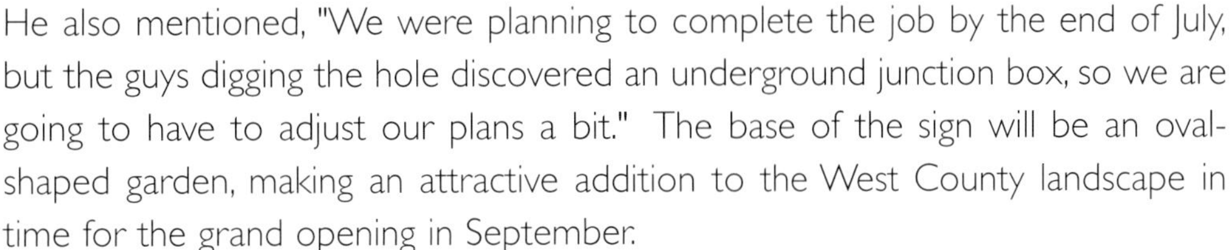

He also mentioned, "We were planning to complete the job by the end of July, but the guys digging the hole discovered an underground junction box, so we are going to have to adjust our plans a bit." The base of the sign will be an oval-shaped garden, making an attractive addition to the West County landscape in time for the grand opening in September.

I worked as a department manager for JCPenney at West County on two different occasions: from 1977-1979 and from 1999-2000. The first time I was transferred from the store, I received as a going away gift a picture of the mall taken from an aerial view, surrounded by the signatures of all the associates. The picture was taken when the mall was brand new, and of course it also shows the Dove. That pic-

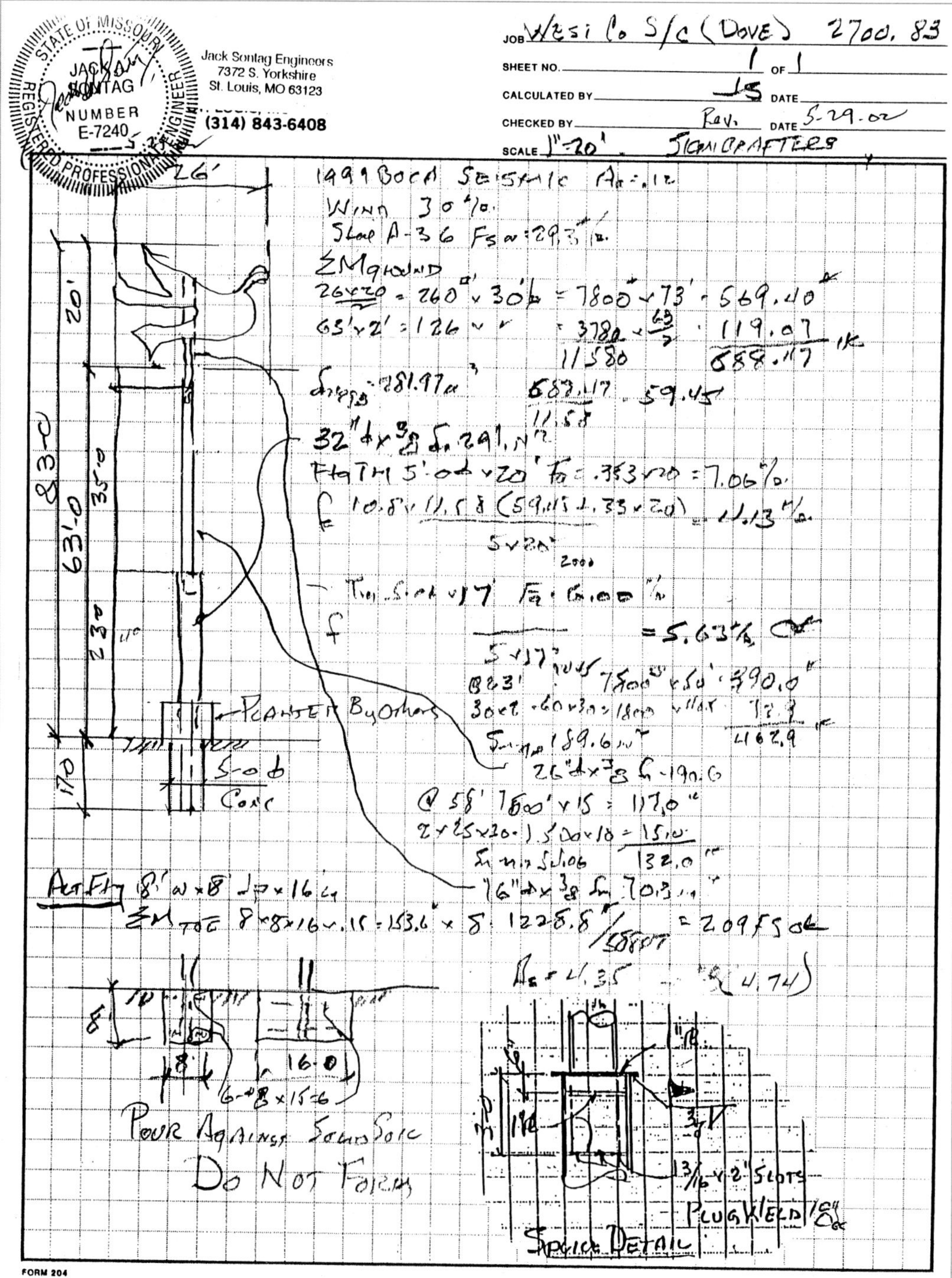

STATE OF MISSOURI
JACK SONTAG
NUMBER
E-7240
REGISTERED PROFESSIONAL ENGINEER

Jack Sontag Engineers
7372 S. Yorkshire
St. Louis, MO 63123
(314) 843-6408

JOB West Co S/C (Dove) 2700.83
SHEET NO. 1 OF 1
CALCULATED BY JS DATE
CHECKED BY Rev. DATE 5-29-02
SCALE 1"=20' SIGNCRAFTERS

1999 BOCA Seismic
Wind 30 #/ft
Steel A-36

Planter By Others
Slab
Conc

Pour Against Solid Soil
Do Not Form

Splice Detail
Plug Weld

FORM 204

Engineering design for 2002 Dove refurbishment.
Courtesy Signcrafters, Inc.

ture is hanging in my office and it brings back many memories, both of people I worked with long ago and also of the mall the way it used to be. The second time I was transferred from the store, I received as my going away gift a 14K gold Dove charm that I wear on a gold chain.

A closer look at the landmark Dove.
Courtesy Westfield Shoppingtown West County

One of my favorite memories of my second time working at that JCPenney was looking out the entrance onto the parking lot (yes, the Dove was in our parking lot, because it was directly outside our store). I saw some of the prettiest sunsets out that door, from our store high on the hill. That view is gone now from JCPenney because of the parking garage, but I guess I can still go to the top level of the garage to get the same view!

I don't know who thought of putting the Dove in the mall when it was first built or what exactly it was supposed to symbolize. But with the state of the world today and even our own country, I think a Dove is exactly the right symbol to have, standing proudly over the mall where thousands of people can see it every day.

Peggy Cooper

Jennifer (O'Keefe) Petrowsky had lots to say about West County. After all, it became her second home during most of her 10-year career in marketing and management. Her career began in 1992 as Marketing Director. By the end of 1993, she moved into position as manager, where she remained until August 4, 2000. She was General Manager of Westfield Shoppingtown West County for nearly seven years.

Repairs after a wind storm were done by Keller Sign Company.
Courtesy Bill and Marge Ryan

According to Petrowsky, the Dove became an icon for the May Centers. The fountains in the mall were designed to inspire the look of a French street in Paris, and from the beginning, the Dove was superimposed in photographs and ads. In response to customer satisfaction surveys, consumers repeatedly referred to West County as "The Dove Mall." It became an icon for the community.

The center was somewhat like a "watering hole" after St. Louis Bread Company opened a store there. "It was like it's own little town," she reflected. "Early in the morning, we had the mall walkers, and they were there faithfully each morning. After their walk, they might sit on the benches and visit or get a morning cup of coffee from the Bread Company. Then later in the morning, the moms would begin to show up with their babies and toddlers. In the afternoon, about 3 P.M., the seniors would come for an afternoon walk, to read, or to just sit on the bench and visit one another."

"I knew them by name," Petrowsky recalls. "We would visit at the same time on the same bench every day. Sometimes when I was out of town, they would let me know they missed me. It was like a community of its own within a larger community. Now that I am no longer there, I really miss that."

In the late 1990's, West County experienced a storm with winds gusting up to 60 miles per hour. Jennifer recalls coming in to work the next morning to hear security's concern, "Something happened to the Dove! Something happened to the Dove!" The wind blew the white panel off one side of the Dove, and it had fallen into pieces along Highway 270.

Fortunately, there were no injuries or damage to motorists driving by. A part of the ballast bulbs were knocked down also. The sign had to be removed by crane and placed on the parking lot. Repairs took several weeks, and many shoppers came to survey the damage and to get a closer look at their treasured bird.

Jennifer recalls that everyone joked, "The Dove was trying to fly away!" After the initial concerns were taken care of, it became a story that brought smiles.

"Without any effort on our part, people became attached to the Dove. It was a trademark," Jennifer noted. "Our ads always included: 'At 270 and Manchester, at the sign of the Dove.' That was an easy identifier, so it was placed on all ads." Many times people would call just to say, "You don't know how important the Dove is to me. I met there to go to camp…or to date…or to go to college…." At least 10 groups per week meeting there would add up to 30 to 40 cars per group. Then when the casinos came, they wanted to have a meeting spot there too. So parking became a problem.

Every year when Mizzou had its first home football game, Jennifer had to present Mr. Africa, the manager from JCPenney, a written security plan. He managed the store for over 10 years, and the Dove was his nemesis. This love-hate relationship was fueled at times when 13 Coach buses parked under the Dove, leaving the riders' cars on the lot. Octoberfest and Mayfest at the wineries and the Mizzou home games generated heavy traffic for parking at West County. Security would have to redirect the traffic so people parked on the southwest corner of the lot or over by Famous-Barr. That way Mr. Africa wouldn't lose parking spaces for his Saturday morning specials at JCPenney.

The Dove awaiting removal in 2001.
Courtesy Westfield Shoppingtown West County

Jennifer recalled, "As part of my 'Dove Parking Security Plan' I took sawhorses with yellow caution tape and secured the area around the Dove until 10 A.M. It had to be in my budget. I would dread Saturdays when Mr. Africa had my pager number and put in 9-1-1 calls for help because there were cars near his entrance to the store."

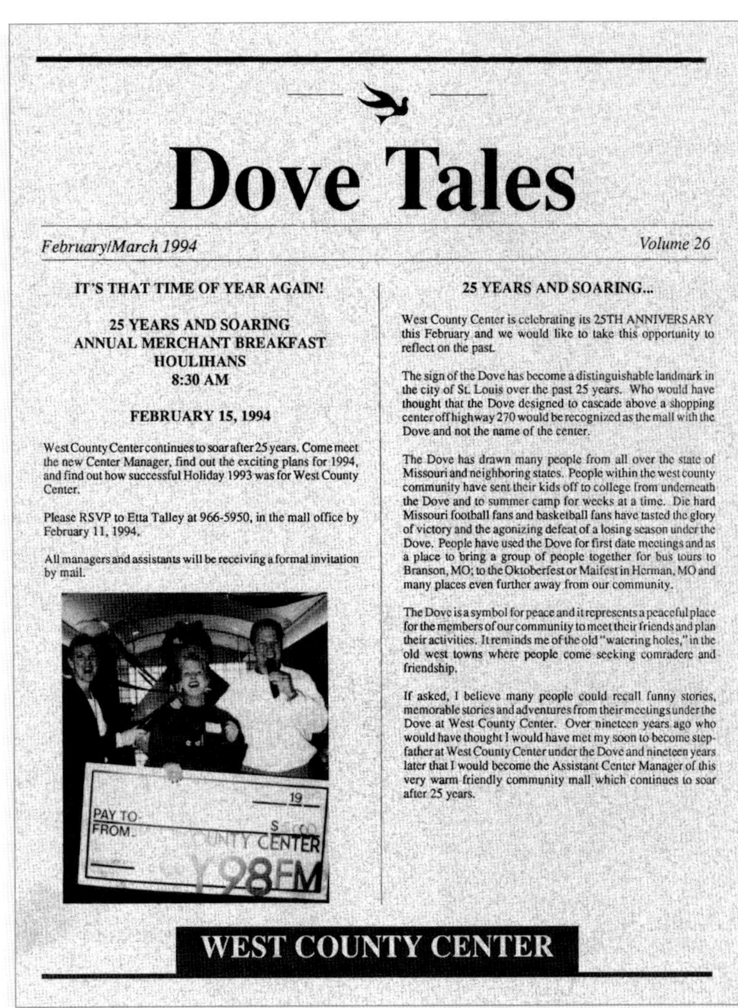

Dove Tales

February/March 1994 *Volume 26*

IT'S THAT TIME OF YEAR AGAIN!

25 YEARS AND SOARING
ANNUAL MERCHANT BREAKFAST
HOULIHANS
8:30 AM

FEBRUARY 15, 1994

West County Center continues to soar after 25 years. Come meet the new Center Manager, find out the exciting plans for 1994, and find out how successful Holiday 1993 was for West County Center.

Please RSVP to Etta Talley at 966-5950, in the mall office by February 11, 1994.

All managers and assistants will be receiving a formal invitation by mail.

25 YEARS AND SOARING...

West County Center is celebrating its 25TH ANNIVERSARY this February and we would like to take this opportunity to reflect on the past.

The sign of the Dove has become a distinguishable landmark in the city of St. Louis over the past 25 years. Who would have thought that the Dove designed to cascade above a shopping center off highway 270 would be recognized as the mall with the Dove and not the name of the center.

The Dove has drawn many people from all over the state of Missouri and neighboring states. People within the west county community have sent their kids off to college from underneath the Dove and to summer camp for weeks at a time. Die hard Missouri football fans and basketball fans have tasted the glory of victory and the agonizing defeat of a losing season under the Dove. People have used the Dove for first date meetings and as a place to bring a group of people together for bus tours to Branson, MO; to the Oktoberfest or Maifest in Herman, MO and many places even further away from our community.

The Dove is a symbol for peace and it represents a peaceful place for the members of our community to meet their friends and plan their activities. It reminds me of the old "watering holes," in the old west towns where people come seeking comradere and friendship.

If asked, I believe many people could recall funny stories, memorable stories and adventures from their meetings under the Dove at West County Center. Over nineteen years ago who would have thought I would have met my soon to become step-father at West County Center under the Dove and nineteen years later that I would become the Assistant Center Manager of this very warm friendly community mall which continues to soar after 25 years.

WEST COUNTY CENTER

Employee publication.
Courtesy Westfield Shoppingtown West County and Jennifer Petrowsky

Jennifer also remembered the merchant communique (newsletter) called "Dove Tales." The logo for the publication was updated in the 1980's, early 1990's, then again in 1994. Jennifer remembered the many center promotions – especially the ones to improve marketing goals to increase traffic and sales in the mall. Readers may remember the campaign, "Rub a Dove, Dove." It was in St. Louis Post Weekly. Customers would come into the center with their ads and rub off the coating to see how many doves they had to determine savings, discounts, and cash prizes. Such promotions made the mall a bustling community.

The Christmas tree that went up under the Dove was quite a project. Even though the lights were inexpensive, the wind would blow the strings, requiring that they be replaced frequently during the holiday season. The hoop at the bottom of the tree was huge – it took four or five men to lift it up. A man on staff named Carl commented to Jennifer when he retired, "You know, Boss, I'm not going to miss putting that tree up under the Dove."

The mayor of Des Peres had the Dove lit up at a designated time during the holidays. It was quite a special occasion. Allen Barklage did his helicopter weather and traffic reports along the stretch of Highway 270 by the mall and always incorporated the Dove into his reports. Jennifer gave a laugh as she remembered the time when the parking lot workers were training their snow plow crews to clean the lot as Barklage was circling around to report the traffic. He added a humorous twist to his report stating, "Can you believe this? They are putting salt out and trucks are plowing West County Center's parking lot – and there is no hint of snow!" That story became a joke for the center staff.

The promotional campaign, "Rub a Dove, Dove," was very successful at increasing traffic and sales at West County.
Courtesy Westfield Shoppingtown West County and Jennifer Petrowsky

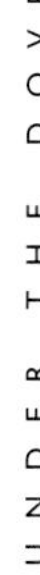

"The Dove helped bridge the connection with the community in times of need and during local and national disasters," Jennifer said. For instance, during the Flood of 1993, a local radio station camped out under the Dove and collected items for flood victims. There were also many recognized news anchors there. For more than 10 years, the Dove was one of the largest drop off sites for Toys for Tots for year-round collections. Many times the center would get calls asking if they took toys. Organizations would camp out for 24 hours and raised more money and collected more toys than at any other location. Meeting under the Dove made it easy to provide a "drive-through drop off" location.

> **Bird Bit**
>
> *How much leasable space was there in the former shopping center?*
>
> •
>
> 563, 621 square feet
>
> •
>
> The new shoppingtown boasts 1.2 million square feet

Petrowsky believed that she was given the task of "the keeper of the Dove," even during negotiations to bring Nordstrom to West County. Every logo designed incorporated the Dove. Petrowsky remembered her role in gathering support to bring in Nordstrom. "When we were pitching for Nordstrom we changed the logo to show the Dove with a red background and white heart. The theme later became a blue heart and white Dove with red border. We managed to capture 10,000 votes in 12 days to show how much we wanted Nordstrom. People came to the center and voted – we had a campaign with t-shirts, buttons, and booths; it was a victory for all of us when Nordstrom agreed to join us. And we literally rolled out the red carpet for the Nordstrom family when they visited. It was quite a presentation, and we were pretty sure they were impressed with our hard work."

"The Dove and I are the same age," Petrowsky said. "I grew up in Manchester and it was the only mall I could go to. I remember going to Woolworth with my grandmother. After I graduated with a bachelor's degree in marketing and public relations, I returned to St. Louis and worked at Mid Rivers Mall in marketing before coming to West County. I remember when I was transferred to West County, my mom was helping me move my office. As we drove toward my new center, mom honked and pointed to the Dove. It really seemed that I was at home

West County was one of the largest drop off sites for Toys for Tots. The Dove became a place where people came for flood relief, book fairs, food drives and other community services and events.
Courtesy Westfield Shoppingtown West County

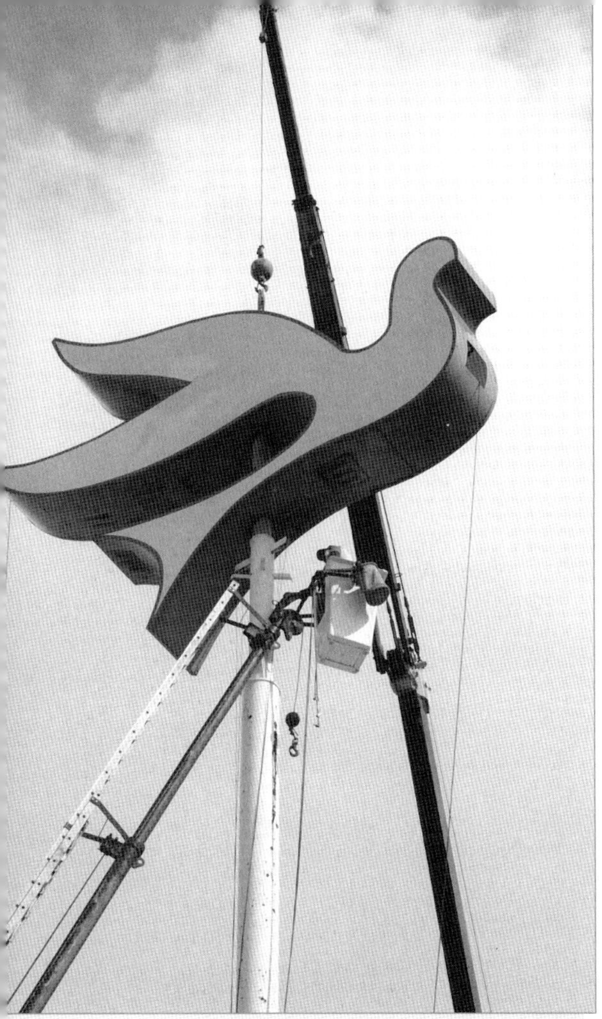

Removal in 2001 for renovation.
Courtesy Westfield Shoppingtown West County

"I saw West County as a stepping stone to a larger mall project, then became entrenched as we pushed for Nordstrom. I would have never guessed that it would take seven years to work out an agreement to bring them here. I knew I wouldn't be here for the new grand opening, but I wanted to help them to reach that goal.

"There was such a feeling of belonging to a community there. It made you feel like part of some small town within a bigger town," she reflected. "I believe that feeling of community can be retained when the center reopens. It can happen through activities and marketing campaigns. The Dove can continue to be part of that."

Seeing the need for future planning took strong leadership in Des Peres. In the 1990's, newer, bigger neighboring malls began to affect West County. As cars no longer filled the parking lot and mall traffic dwindled, mall management and local government teamed up to reverse the growing trend. It was the work of the Board of Aldermen under the mayoral leadership of Sharon Burkhardt from 1992-2000 that change began to happen rapidly.

Burkhardt recalls telling the board, "You can go forward or you can go backward, but you can't stand still." She pioneered change after Westfield purchased the outdated mall. "I watched this mall go from being the number one mall in the late sixties to becoming the oldest and smallest mall in the region. It was time for a change."

Sharon recalls that the board was divided about what should happen since the land did not belong to the city, but rather to Westfield. "It is as though I would go into your home and tell you I don't like your kitchen, and proceed to tell you how to redecorate or change the design. So we could only suggest what might be in everyone's best interest. After all, board members serve to protect the people in the community. We disagreed a lot, but there was one thing we unanimously agreed on – we needed to keep the Dove!"

Des Peres guaranteed the residents that the mall owners would not buy out homes or grow beyond its property line. The city hired attorneys to work with twelve volunteers, the Planning and Zoning Commission, to ensure that the residents of the community were central to the plans for Westfield's new center. The process took almost three years, according to Burkhardt. She also worked with the highway department to accommodate the growing traffic problem, because she saw an opportunity to get highway department funding for roads. This was a step that helped to prepare Des Peres for the growth in the traffic with an updated mall while sparing the expense to local government and businesses.

Westfield and the West County community provided a warm welcome to the Nordstrom family during negotiations.
Courtesy Westfield Shoppingtown West County and Jennifer Petrowsky

How did the city and Westfield manage to entice Nordstrom to move into town? May Company's Famous-Barr first had to agree to allow Nordstrom into the area, since a previous contract prohibited the competition from moving into the region. Finally, May Company realized that without a new name in town, the center might not have been positioned for success in competing with neighboring malls. In 1996, the doors were opened for negotiations to invite Norstrom into the new center.

Burkhardt noted that the Nordstrom brothers, the original owners, were preparing to retire and hand off the company to its next generation of family members. This acquisition for Des Peres and Westfield actually became the younger generation's first "deal" for the family, so it was a celebration everyone could share. The negotiations brought out the best in everyone, and the support of the city government was impressive. Westfield brought in its top executives from as far away as Australia to join in conversations with the Nordstrom family.

When the negotiations with Nordstrom were nearly complete in 1996, Burkhardt called the board together for what everyone thought was the big announcement that their answer was "yes." Unfortunately, her news was quite different, and she announced that she would be leaving temporarily to begin a new battle – fighting chronic myelogenous leukemia. She left for treatment in Seattle, Washington, at which time Rick Lahr took over during her absence. The support of her family and the entire community was evident through the blood and bone marrow drives, and the celebration that welcomed her home after the disease was in remission. Her life expectancy was less than two years upon diagnosis, yet she has been living cancer-free for five years.

(Bottom photo, left to right) During the 1996 campaign to bring Nordstrom, Marketing Director Jana Carani, Mayor Sharon Burkhardt, and General Manager Jennifer (O'Keefe) Petrowsky team up. They ran a successful campaign to encourage customers to shop under the Dove at the new Westfield Shoppingtown West County.

Courtesy Westfield Shoppingtown West County and Jennifer Petrowsky

Burkhardt would have never guessed what the future would hold in the sixties as she and her fiance at the time, Ron, met under the Dove when they traveled from opposite directions to meet for dates. She remembers the small four-lane road that Highway 270 once was and that the Dove was the only landmark in the region.

"The city of Des Peres outlawed pole signs, but they made the Dove an exception because it was such a landmark; people insisted that it should stay," Burkhardt noted. "It was an important landmark back in the sixties when I was dating the man I eventually married, and it still is today. Today, more than 30 years later, the Dove still brings back great memories. In fact, we can even see it out of our window upstairs here at home. It holds a lot of meaning."

Her work as mayor benefited the community because of both her professional abilities and her personal experience while in office. She helped to move the community toward a unified goal. The benefits will be evident for years to come as the future brings growth to businesses in Des Peres.

The Dove, resting before a long ride to General Sign Company in Cape Girardeau.
Courtesy Westfield Shoppingtown West County

The ordinance that banned all signs with the exception of the Dove.
Courtesy City of Des Peres

(G) Comprehensive Sign Plan

A Comprehensive Sign Plan shall be approved by the Board of Aldermen following review by the Planning & Zoning Commission prior to issuance of any permits for construction of signs other than traffic directional signs and temporary construction signs as permitted by the code. Such Comprehensive Sign Plan shall, at a minimum, conform to the following requirements:

1. No outdoor advertising signs or "commander/reader board" signs shall be permitted on the site. Provided, however, temporary signs approved by the Board of Aldermen may be utilized in conjunction with special events including the grand opening of the shopping center.

2. Only one (1) pole sign shall be permitted and shall be placed along the frontage along the Interstate highway and such sign shall incorporate the center's trademark logo (The Dove).

Some people from local churches used to tell us that the Dove represented the Holy Spirit, but in fact it was simply a symbolic design. The Public Relations and Communications Department had many phone calls, inquiries, and complaints each business day. One call in particular was surprising.

During the 1980's, the center was remodeled. At the grand reopening, entertainment was provided to occupy the many children who accompanied their parents. One such entertainer was a magician who was noted for his amazing talents. A call was placed to complain that this type of entertainment was evil; that magic was intended to undermine the work of the Holy Spirit, whom the mall was representing – and the Dove was proof of that. This was a very surprising complaint, since there was never an intent to offend anyone, but rather to entertain children as their parents took a look at the newly decorated mall.

This symbol represented a destination as well as a point of departure. The West County Dove was a meeting spot to head off for college, and to return as well, and it was an essential location that everyone knew.

Randy Smith
WESTFIELD CORPORATION

Former mayor Jody Griggs provided this special edition of the West Suburban Journals with articles by Regina DeLuca, Staff writer.

PROGRESS '94

Looking to the Future

Wednesday, February 23, 1994

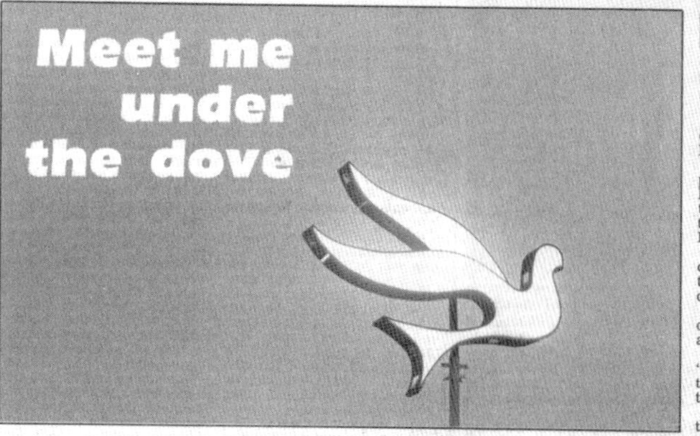

Enduring symbol lights above mall

By Regina DeLuca
Staff writer

With the releasing of 125 homing pigeons in front of an audience of 5,000, West County Center in Des Peres opened its doors on Feb. 21, 1969.

Since then, the dove soaring atop its 65-foot pylon has become a symbol of the center and a landmark for the community. It flies high above the shopping center at Interstate 270 (or at the time of its opening, Interstate 244) and Manchester Road.

While there may be some speculation as to who conceived the big bird, or why, one thing is certain: it definitely dovetailed as a symbol of the center.

"Who would have thought it would have caught on?" said Jennifer O'Keefe, assistant center manager. "People call us the mall with the dove.

"People meet under the dove," O'Keefe said. "Diehard Mizzou fans meet under the dove, so they've tasted victory and agonized over defeat there.

"People even send their kids off to college under the dove."

> **"The dove faces westward, so it was symbolic of growth moving westward."**
>
> Jody Griggs
> Former Des Peres mayor

Jody Griggs, former Des Peres alderwoman and mayor, remembers when the dove first went up.

"We really had a lot of growth on Manchester Road (in the 1960s)," Griggs recalls. "The dove faces westward, so it was symbolic of growth moving westward."

Doing a little digging herself into the origin of the dove, Griggs said the dove may have been chosen as a symbol of peace, love and security.

And all adjectives hold true, Griggs said.

"The other night when there was a lot of fog and we were driving home, I knew we weren't far," Griggs said. "I said, 'Hey, I see the bird, we can't be far from home.' "

Flying high: Dove, mall celebrate 25 years

By Regina DeLuca
Staff writer

From an idea hatched a quarter of a century ago, the big dove still soars high above the shopping center and community it was created to watch over.

At the time West County Center was built, it was the only shopping center in the area. Since then, a flock of others have migrated to town, but as West County Center celebrates it 25th anniversary, it remains a focal point in the community.

The site of the center was an attraction even before the mall was built. People came from miles around to watch images fly across the big screen when the Manchester Drive-In theater occupied the grounds at Manchester Road and Interstate 270.

The Manchester Drive-In was the first drive-in theater in St. Louis.

Although more than 25 years have passed since then, Mary Landvatter of Ballwin still recalls seeing her first drive-in movie at the theater. The movie was "The Three Stooges in Orbit."

"I had nightmares after watching that movie," said Landvatter, a 23-year employee of JC Penney, one of the two department stores anchoring the mall. Famous-Barr is the other.

Landvatter also remembers attending Easter sunrise service at the drive-in.

Families would gather early Easter morning and hook speakers on their car windows to hear the preacher's sermon.

Landvatter's association with the site continues after the big screen was torn down and the white dove went up. On a whim, she took a job fresh out of high school selling housewares at JC Penney.

Over the years, Landvatter witnessed several changes at the center — JC Penney in particular. "We had some different departments than we do now," Landvatter said.

The store's former pet department caused quite a flap for Landvatter and her co-workers. "The birds would get out, and we'd have to chase them with a net," she said.

Several departments went the way of the specialty stores, but Landvatter said she won't be leaving. "I probably always will be here," she said.

And that's a good thing.

"We get a lot of local people who shop here, a lot of the same customers," Landvatter said. "I see the same customers and they say to me, 'God, you've been here a long time.' "

Like Landvatter, Jim Vuch of south county has some stories to tell.

Vuch has worked at Boyd's — now Boyd's Graham and Gunn — specialty clothing store for some time now.

"Probably since 1947, but I quit counting," said the 64-year-old semiretired Vuch. He's been at West County Center site for more than 10 years.

The farmland right across from the new mall 25 years ago and what was then a two-lane Interstate 270 are just part of what Vuch remembers when the center was first constructed.

"The decor, when this mall was built, was called Old World style," Vuch said. "The whole mall took on a Paris street with lights, fountains when the mall was first built. It looked like you were walking down a French street."

After a quarter of a century, West County Center remains a focal point in the community. Many west countians remember watching movies at the site when it was the Manchester Drive-In, and some recall Easter sunrise services at the drive-in.

Rick Graefe photos

See CENTER, Page 6

MAYOR

Sharon Burkhardt
734 Stump Road
965-6684

CITY ADMINISTRATOR

Douglas Harms
City Hall
966-4600

ALDERMEN

WARD I

Stephen Wicker
1555 Windridge Drive
965-5642

John Parker
11951 Devonshire
966-0204

WARD II

W.O. (Jim) Gilmour
2345 Hollyhead Drive
822-4085

Rick Lahr
630 Dougherty View Ct.
965-5058

WARD III

James Doering
2114 Ballas View
821-0872

Charles E. Wetzel, Jr.
5 Ranch Lane
966-5961

VOLUME VI ISSUE II **FEBRUARY 1994**

SNOW REMOVAL

The 1993/1994 snow removal season is upon us, and the conditions are indeed unique. So far, holidays have been the key dates for snow and ice, and cold temperatures have been the rule. As of January 17, crews have fought 6 snow and ice storms but only 11 inches of snow. The e
low temperatures following the storms ha
removal difficult. As a result, over 370 to
and 2500 gallons of calcium chloride ha
utilized already. In a normal season, w
expect only 8 storms all year totaling a
inches of snow requiring use of 400 tons o
3000 gallons of calcium chloride. Thi
indeed shaping up to be an unusual one.

The Department of Public Works is
ible for combating snow and ice from n
miles of City streets (public and private
City facilities. Under unusual circumstan
crews also pitch in and help the State anc
on Manchester Road, Ballas Road and De
Ferry Road, if they fall behind schedul
streets become hazardous.

The City has developed a SNOW PLA
divides the community into 5 sectors and
priority on heavily-traveled streets and ma
Our goal is to keep the streets safe and pa
all times and to achieve clear pavement fro
to-curb within twelve (12) hours after the en
storm.

The main problem that crews exper
snow removal is vehicles parked on street
cially narrow streets and cul-de-sacs! If y
park on the street, avoid cul-de-sacs and do
opposite another car. Please be aware
location of FIRE HYDRANTS and STOR
TER INLETS and don't pile snow in front o
Finally, please keep all sidewalks in front of your home or business clean of ice and snow to make walking safer for pedestrians.

While our 11 employees from the Street and Park Divisions physically man our snowplows, snow removal is a TEAM EFFORT including the

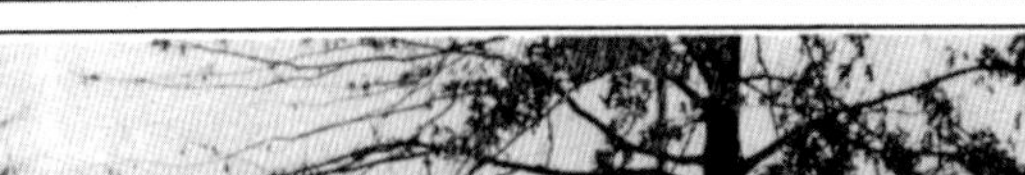

West County Center Celebrates 25 Years

Residents are invited to join the managment and tenants of West County Shopping Center in celebrating 25 years of service to the community on Wednesday, February 23rd at 11:30 AM in the court at West County Center.

years of service to the
community on Wednes-
day, February 23rd at
11:30 AM in the court at
West County Center.

Des Peres celebrated the Dove's 25th year in West County.
Courtesy City of Des Peres

Chapter 4

Love Under the Dove

As long as the Dove is there, so too shall our memories, our love, and our love story be there as well.

Andre Edwards

To some, the Dove seemed to be an ideal place for a romantic rendezvous. Why was that so? After all, it was not exactly a discreet location for parking. However, it was easy to locate when making a "love connection." Many couples met there before heading off on dates, and some eventually married. Late night visitors to that spot were frequently asked to leave by the Des Peres Police Department and Westfield security. This chapter offers readers a glimpse into the lives of some of the couples who found love under the Dove.

My parents invited three field workers from my dad's church to their home, and that's where I met Jim on January 9, 1976. I liked him immediately, even though I was planning to return to California to be with the man I had been dating there. Our first meeting on that day in January changed everything! I never returned to California, but rather stayed in St. Louis and soon fell in love with Jim. His kindness, compassion, commitment to his faith, and sense of humor swept me away.

Jim and Laurie Schack, 1976.
Courtesy Laurie Schack

We dated for a month, and by the end of January, we knew we were in love. I will never forget going to the shopping center under the Dove on February 14. Jim told his mother that I was the one he was going to marry, and she gave him a pin with five diamonds from his grandmother to use in designing a ring for me.

I remember referring to West County simply as "the Dove," because I identified with the symbol, which meant something very special for me. That day we went to Wehmueller Jewelers to order our wedding set. I remember telling Sarah, my sister, about my plans before I told anyone else, because I was so excited, but everything was happening so fast! We were engaged on March 17 and married on August 14 that same year.

Today we are still very much in love, and have celebrated 26 years of marriage with our three beautiful children. Whenever we drive by the Dove, it brings a flood of memories and sentiment, just as though it happened yesterday. My engagement was a very special time in my life.

Laurie Schack

According to the Grand Times, a Jefferson County Publication, our story had Valentine charm that made it good enough to publish in February 2002:

Shirley, 65, and Dan Daniels, 69, of Arnold are still newlyweds after an arranged meeting by Internet on a site for senior citizens. Their names were matched after each answered a series of questions about their interests, background, etc. After they were *matched, they had a five-month period to continue screening one another, before eventually meeting…under the Dove.*

"As soon as we met, we knew. The sparks flew," Dan recalls. They celebrated their first anniversary on May 2, 2002. Is it different the second time around? "We had been through bad times, and we weren't going to make the same mistakes we did the first time around," says Dan.

As of February 2002, Dan has 10 grandchildren and four great grandchildren and Shirley has 25 grandchildren and four great-grandchildren. "This is a different time, a different year, and a different world – and we are so deeply in love." It all began under the Dove!

Danny Daniels

How could I forget our first date on March 17, 1999? My grandmother worked with Michael for around nine years, and finally talked us into a blind date. Our first conversation on the phone lasted for hours, so we felt both excited and nervous about our first meeting. We planned to meet under the Dove before heading off to play racquetball. To ease the nervous tension, we decided to walk around Westfield for awhile. We never made it onto the racquetball court, but rather ended up going to dinner and visiting under the Dove until the early hours of the next morning!

Exactly one year later, we were running errands on a rainy day before going out to eat. As we pulled onto the parking lot at Westfield, Michael headed over to the Dove. We immediately aroused the suspicion of a security guard who began circling around us. Michael turned off the engine, and suggested that we get out of the car. Suddenly I knew something was up, and got a nervous feeling in my stomach. He took my hand as I moved from the car, and he dropped to his knees as he proposed. The rain nicely disguised the tearful moment as he placed the ring on my finger. I couldn't believe it! I just hugged him. We were too excited to eat, so we rushed to tell our parents the good news instead.

Meeting under the Dove led to wedding bells for many couples. Michael and Christine Foster used the Dove for their wedding program, place settings and their wedding cake.
Courtesy Christine Foster

Christine Lisa Welsch
and
Michael Christopher Foster

"This is my beloved, and this is my friend."
Song of Solomon 5:16

We got married exactly two years after we first met under the Dove. We just had to somehow incorporate the Dove into our wedding because it evokes so much sentiment. The Dove was used on our invitations, for decorations, and as a topper on our wedding cake! Every time we drive by Westfield we are reminded of where we began our life together. For our future anniversaries we plan to visit our special place under the Dove.

Michael and Christine Foster

It was a beautiful fall evening. The smell of burning leaves filled the air. The leaves tumbled over the shopping mall parking lot, scraping the concrete before nestling together as they awaited the next gust of wind to blow them around again.

I was 16 years old and just finished watching my boyfriend play football at a private high school. We lived in different areas. He lived near the airport and I lived near Grant's Farm in Crestwood. We would always meet halfway, under the Dove, and walk around the shopping mall as we held hands and talked about our different schools. Afterwards, we would stand under the Dove where we always parked our cars.

We were in love and nothing in the world mattered to us. We were blind to all of the shoppers scurrying in and out of the stores, in search of early Christmas presents.

The white Dove stood graciously above us as we leaned against our cars gazing into each others' eyes. As he leaned in to give me an ever-so-soft kiss, my heart raced. Then it happened...my first kiss...that stopped my world from turning. To this day, I remember looking up into the sky and seeing the beautiful, white Dove as it illuminated the parking lot.

Jean Marie Baker

Bird Bit

How many parking spaces are under the Dove at the new Westfield Shoppingtown West County?

•

5,553

Chapter 5

Family Memories

I went to college at the University of Tulsa, and there were many of us who would come home for holidays. Many times we all met under the Dove to head back to school. I still remember cramming into a station wagon, hugging our parents good-bye, and heading out.

Trish Washburn Gunby

It is increasingly difficult to pass family traditions from one generation to the next. With a whirlwind of change around us, things seem to rarely stay the same. Looking back with nostalgia on our special memories, we may want to recreate those experiences for our children. Bringing the past traditions to the present and future generations can be a treasured gift. Many times those traditions can be as simple as a shopping trip, or a memory of driving past the Dove. This chapter offers readers family memories that many writers have shared about their excursions to West County.

Our family memories under the Dove actually began long before it was there. I remember going with my family to the Manchester Drive-In. Before the movie started, we would take my little sister to the playground just in front of the screen and let her play while waiting for the movie to begin. As I got a little older, I remember going to the drive-in on dates, but not very often, as it was quite a distance to drive from where we lived in the city.

After the center was built, my mother and I would meet my sister there every Thursday. It became a tradition, even as our children came along. We would all meet at the center, look in the stores, and then stop at Seven Kitchens for lunch.

Before the days of car seats, my kids would stand on the floor in the back seat of the car and look out the front window for the "shopping Bird." My oldest son, Christopher, was fascinated by the Dove. When we found out they were going to take it down during construction, he asked me to take some pictures of it just in case they changed it or it didn't return.

(Left to right) Melissa, Christopher, and Michael Olsen paid a visit to Santa during the 1975 holiday season at West County.
Courtesy Judy Olsen

There were times we never bought anything on our shopping trips, but at some time or another, I'm sure we were in every store. I know we always went to Famous, JCPenney, and a store that sold ties. Sometimes they had two-dollar ties. My mother was always shopping for ties for my father. We regularly shopped at Woolworth, where Grandma bought Little Golden Books or matchbox cars for the boys. Usually the kids had a dollar to spend – that was when you could really get something for a dollar.

Our last stop was lunch at Seven Kitchens, and we sat and visited before heading home. The kids always had a hotdog. One time my son, Chris, wanted an ice cream cone and Grandma gave him the money to buy it. He was too shy to ask, so his not-so-shy little sister stepped up to the counter, reached up with the money, and announced, "Chris wants an ice cream cone." I am sure the man behind the counter could see nothing more than her little hand!

As the kids got older and started school, our trips became less frequent, but we will always have fond memories of those days we spent on our shopping trips. These were special times spent with family.

Judy Olsen

My mother, Marlene Buren, suffers from an unpredictable mental illness called manic depression. She has been in and out of mental hospitals.

I recall one year when my mom was being treated in St. Vincent DePaul Hospital. My Grandma and I would always drive past the Westfield Shopping Center and notice the Dove. It seemed to look graceful and free, and we wished that my Mom could feel that way too. My Grandma began calling the landmark "Marlene's Dove." It has become a symbol of hope in my family. I felt that it was a real loss that they took it down, and look forward to seeing it again.

Barb Buren

In 1971, I was working at Missouri Baptist Medical Center. At the time Bill Runyan, M.D., was an orthopedic surgery resident at Barnes-Jewish Hospital and donated time at Shriners Hospital. His wife, Lola, worked with me in the laboratory, and we became good friends. Their daughter, Laura, was five years old at the time. To her, West County Center became the Big Bird Mall, and the name stuck with us even after their move back to Little Rock in 1972. The Runyans returned once since 1972, and we met at the Big Bird Mall before heading to Houlihan's for lunch.

In 1999, after dedicating his life to medicine, Bill was diagnosed with cancer and died. Laura is grown and has two children of her own. She is planning a trip back to the Big Bird Mall and the St. Louis Zoo with her children.

Bird Bit

How many cars have passed in front of the Dove on Highway 270 since it was originally installed in 1969?

•

A. 2 billion

•

B. 1.3 billion

•

C. 5 billion

•

According to the Missouri Department of Transportation reports on annual average daily traffic, between 1969 and 2000, approximately 1.3 billion cars passed Manchester as they traveled in both directions on Highway 270.

When my daughter, Kimberly, was born in 1972, we took many trips to what we had come to know as the Big Bird Mall. As she grew older, it became her meeting place for catching rides to and from college. The bird was taken down while she was expecting her son, Kurtis. We are looking forward to carrying on the tradition when the mall reopens.

It will be great to see the Big Bird watching us once again.

Carolyn Hampel

One cold Saturday in 2001, I stood with my husband and a handful of others, mostly mall representatives and Des Peres officials, to watch the de-lighting of the Dove, formerly the symbol of West County Center. I was thrilled to think there would be a big new shopping center so near to my Kirkwood home. That mall has been a big part of my life over the years.

In 1969, as a young bride expecting my first baby, I attended the opening of the center.

I wandered through the baby department, trying to visualize a real baby using the bright daisy-decorated items we chose at Famous-Barr. The photography studio on the lower level was the site of my baby girl's first official photo. At Christmas she had her first introduction (unfortunately tearful) to Santa. In the years to come we all stood outside excitedly to await his arrival led by a Parkway High School band.

In 1974, our second daughter was born, and official photo sessions were moved to JCPenney Studio – first on the main floor and then on the lower level. JCPenney was the one-stop shop not only for baby photos, but also for a three-year-old's dance leotard and eventually, Brownie uniforms.

Our shopping sprees often included lunch at A&W Root Beer, or later Hot Dogs 'n More, and a brief stroll down the mall. Woolworth and Kaybee Toys were great stops for treats and toys. Eventually at the age of 13, the girls visited Wehmueller Jewelers for ear piercing. West County always had the latest teen fashions to fill their wish lists for Christmas and birthdays. Stores such as Contempo, The Gap, and Express were sure to have just what I was looking for.

Each year Santa ushered in holiday festivities at West County.
Courtesy Westfield Shoppingtown West County

Meetings at the Dove were the highlight of our summers in the seventies when cousins visited from St. Charles. The mall made a great art gallery for children's paintings and drawings as well as a performing arts mecca for school district choirs and bands. When my girls were old enough to work, the mall also became a place of employment.

West County marked many milestones as our girls grew up and graduated from college. Now they have launched their careers, and West County became our

Bird Bit

When did the center close for renovations?

•

January 27, 2001, just days away from its 32nd birthday. The center opened its doors on February 5, 1969, with a grand opening later that month.

•

The reopening date: September 20, 2002

partner in wedding planning and shopping. In fact, our last trip to the mall before it closed was to purchase an outfit for the bridal shower.

I think there is a saying, "Life, death, and rebirth...." That is why we were at the official closing and we hope to attend reopening ceremonies in September 2002. Shopping at West County has been a big part of our family life. The officials have promised replicas of the Dove in the new Westfield Shoppingtown West County – so we'll see you there!

Nancy Latt

My memories are of simple things such as meeting friends under the Dove for a movie or to go on a float trip. West County Center was the first place our parents would allow my friends and me to go shopping on our own. We would walk the mall as if we were really grown up, have lunch, visit the teen stores, and eventually work our way into JCPenney to try on wigs. Our parents would pick us up outside JCPenney at the door closest to the Dove.

My favorite memories are of taking my small children to the West County Center. We would pick up their grandmother, Sunny (now deceased), and go there for lunch, then to shop. They always asked if we were going "to the mall with the Bird." When we would drive down the highway they would often shout out, "Look, Mommy, the mall with the Bird!"

My children are now 15 and 12 years old, and they will sometimes refer to it as the "mall with the Bird where we used to go shopping with Sunny." It is often a catalyst for fun trips down memory lane.

Mary Fava

When I think about the Dove in West County, I cannot help but think about my (wonderful, amazing) mom. I grew up in South County and went to a private high school in Webster Groves. Until I could drive myself, I had to make carpool arrangements to social outings, play rehearsals, and all of my other activities. To make matters worse, most of my friends at the time lived a considerable distance from my house. So each weekend of my first year of high school, I faced the same transportation dilemma: "How am I going to get there?"

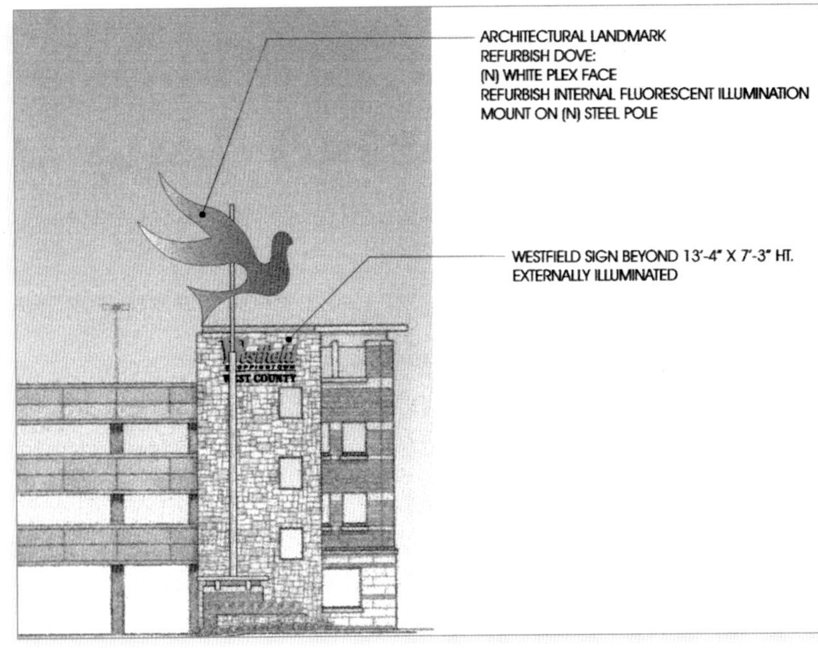

Rendering for the new Westfield Dove, 2002.
Courtesy Westfield Shoppingtown West County and City of Des Peres.

I was the oldest of five children, so it was often quite a task for my parents to schedule our events and plans. When I wanted to meet my friends, my mom's standard response to their parents was to meet us under the Dove since it was central.

When I turned 16 and began driving, it seemed that I got lost no matter where I was headed! Every trip took nearly an hour longer than it would for anyone else. My mom always insisted that I meet my friends under the Dove to avoid this problem, so most of my weekend adventures began there. At the time I wondered if my mom had some sort of obsession with the Dove. Why did she always arrange plans at the Dove? Why did the Dove seem to have such influence?

When I heard about this book and began to think about my own "Dove stories," I realized how significant it is in the St. Louis area. I also became aware of my own respect and admiration for the Dove. I remember how it looked through the eyes of a child in the backseat of the car – mysterious and graceful. I asked my mom about it when we passed, thinking it stood for something holy like the dove in the Noah's Ark story. It was more of a landmark for me than the Arch, because we drove past it quite often.

The Dove also reminds me of those car rides with my mom as a child. As the oldest child, I would frequently sit in the front seat – the one closest to my mom. I loved long car rides, and at that young age, every car ride seemed long!

Those rides gave me the opportunity to really connect with my mom, and she was always fun to ride with. She would lead sing-a-longs or tell stories. On vacation, both of my parents invented games to make the ride more enjoyable. I wanted those rides to last as long as possible. When I saw the Dove in the sky, I knew that we were almost home, and I was relieved that we still had a little more time to be together. I would try to stay awake so I could enjoy my time with mom, especially if everyone else was asleep in the back.

The Dove stands in the background of many of my memories. I am moving out of town, and there are so many things about St. Louis that I will miss, most of all my family and friends. I look forward to my trips back to St. Louis when I can tell my mom to meet me under the Dove…at Nordstrom!

Rachel (Lang) Elliott

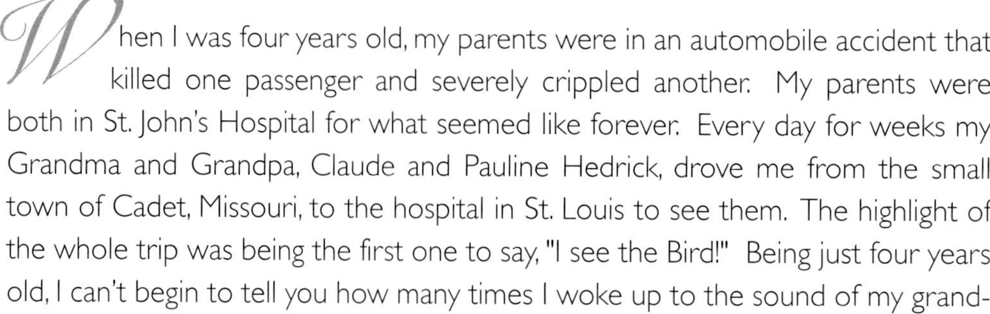

When I was four years old, my parents were in an automobile accident that killed one passenger and severely crippled another. My parents were both in St. John's Hospital for what seemed like forever. Every day for weeks my Grandma and Grandpa, Claude and Pauline Hedrick, drove me from the small town of Cadet, Missouri, to the hospital in St. Louis to see them. The highlight of the whole trip was being the first one to say, "I see the Bird!" Being just four years old, I can't begin to tell you how many times I woke up to the sound of my grandpa's voice, laughing, and saying, "I see the Bird! Guess I saw it first!" I'd get so mad!!

Krystal Farley

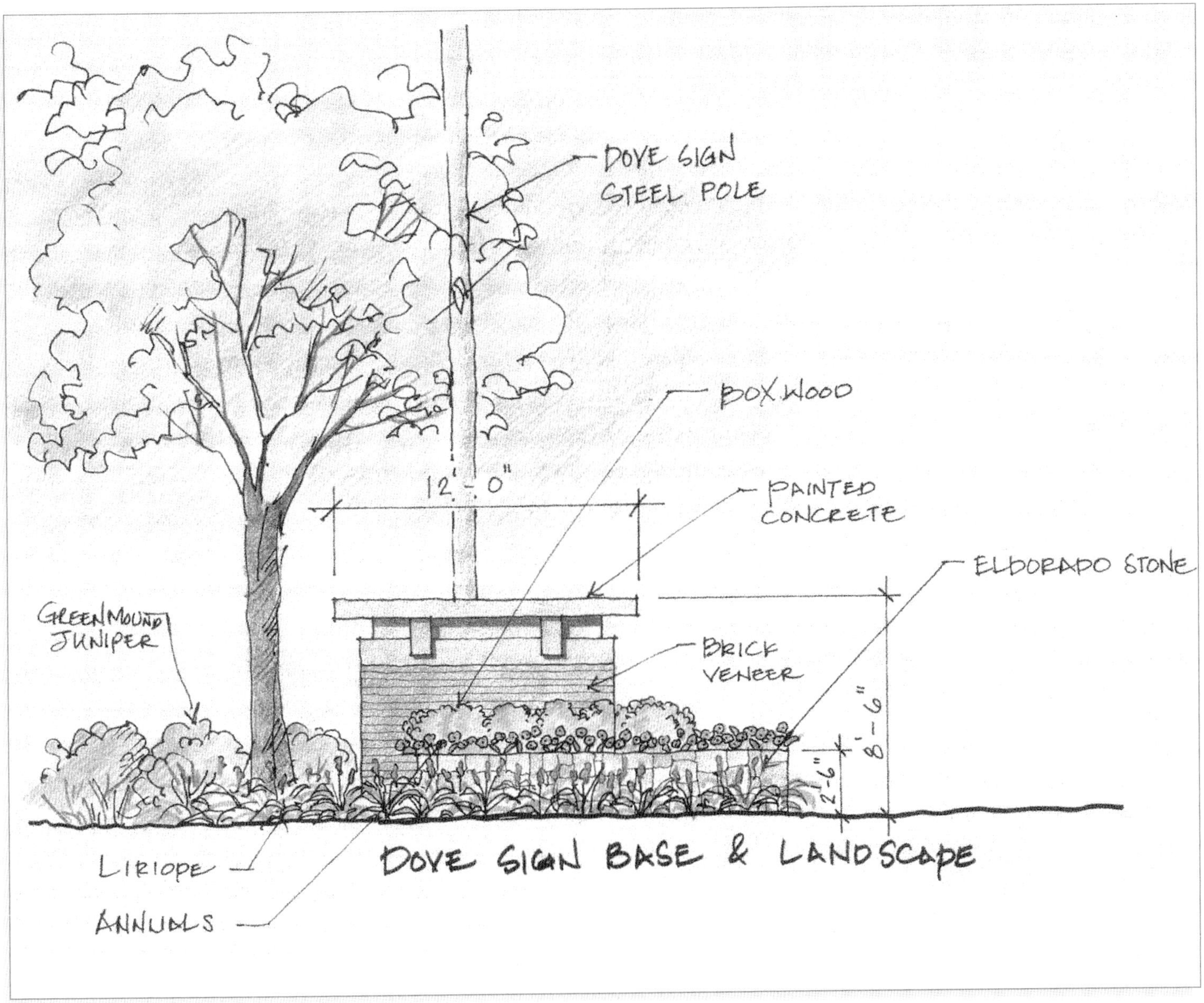

Rendering for the new Westfield Dove, 2002.
Courtesy Westfield Shoppingtown West County and City of Des Peres.

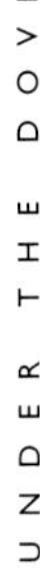

When I was very young, I was a Blue Bird. This was an organization similar to the Brownies and Girl Scouts. When my father and I would travel north on Highway 270 to visit his colleague in Clayton, we would pass West County Center. As we passed the Dove, my father would announce, "There's Blue Bird Headquarters."

Now that I am over 40 years old, I still fondly remember my father's words as I pass the Dove…the "Blue Bird Headquarters."

Lauren Erger

What type of lighting has been used in the Dove through the years?

•

The original sign used cold cathode tubing, which was soon replaced by fluorescent tubing

•

In 1986, those lights were replaced by mercury vapor

•

In 2002, mercury vapor will be used

I lived in Old Maryland Heights and my four boys were born from 1954 through 1963. When we first noticed the Dove, we happened to drive by and David, our oldest son, said, "Look at the ghost!" Could it have been around the time of Halloween? Possibly. But I tried to tell him that it was a Dove so it would not frighten his younger brothers. It was no use. So for our family, it has always been "the ghost." When our boys were old enough to drive, I gave directions …if Manchester Road was part of it, the boys would always say, "You mean the Ghost Street?" It was always a great place to meet friends, "under the Dove."

Now that I live South, I really miss our ghost! Thanks for bringing it back.

Mary Flotron

I remember once when our family was driving home from vacation when I was about six years old. I didn't know if we were close to home or not – so I just kept looking out the window. Then I saw the Dove, and I thought to myself, "That Dove is close to my house." So I knew I would soon be home.

Mike Mertzlufft, Grade 7

When my two children were quite small, my parents lived in Pevely, Missouri, and quite often would want to meet for lunch and visit with the kids.

Pevely, 50 or so miles away from St. Louis, was quite a drive for an inexperienced driver such as myself with small children. Knowing I was rather nervous about where to exit, my father said, "Drive on 270 and when you see the Dove, that's the shopping center where we will be at. We will meet you by the show."

As we all know during trips in the car, children always ask, "Are we there yet?" With my father's expert directions, I would tell my kids that when they see the Dove they would be with Grampa and Gramma very soon.

Sally Wheeler

I remember meeting my rides to and from Rockhurst College in 1985 and 1986 at "the Dove Mall," as my family called it. This was a strong, memorable time in my life.

Michelle Graham Martin

On May 25, 1993, I was having lunch with a co-worker, Craig Wielansky, at the St. Louis Bread Company in the mall. I was eight months pregnant with my first child, and as I stood up to leave, my water broke – right there in the restaurant! Not only was I totally embarrassed, but my shoes and my bright red dress were soaked.

Craig was quite understanding, being the father of two, and offered to get the car and pick me up at the entrance. I cleaned myself up, and proceeded to walk through the mall as my shoes squished all the way to the door. "Oh my goodness," I panicked. "I am going to deliver my baby – and *a month early!*"

Craig drove me to St. John's Mercy Medical Center, and my husband met us there. My beautiful daughter was born that afternoon, and we named her Culver Marie Randolph. The name Culver means "Dove" and it is also my maiden name. Today, Culver is almost nine years old, and every time we drive by Westfield Shoppingtown West County, we talk about the Dove and how it is "her" mall. We were sad when it was taken down, but plan to share in the celebration when it comes back!

Rebecca Randolph

When I was younger, my mom always took me to West County. I didn't know where we were going in the car, but whenever I saw the Dove, I knew where we were. Since the Dove meant we were going to the mall, I automatically associated all shopping malls with the Dove.

I still had this notion in my head when my family and I took a trip to Kansas City to visit my aunt and uncle. While we were in Kansas City, we stopped at numerous shopping malls. While there, I would not be satisfied until I saw the Dove. Needless to say, I was very upset quite often!

When I returned home, my mom and I again traveled out to West County. When I saw the Dove, the symbol of West County, the symbol of our great city, I was so happy. I must have had a smile on my face the rest of the day. As I sat in the car for the ride home, I realized what I had seen that day. Although I had traveled away from home, I realized that nothing could take the place of the Dove and my hometown. After all, there's no place like home!

Daniel Hrdlicka, Grade 7

Years ago, our daughter, Laurie, and her husband, Brian, moved to Springfield, Missouri, with our grandson Shaun. Shaun was three months old at the time.

They visited us quite often and Shaun learned to say "Papa" and "Gammaw." At that same time, when he was two years old, he also came to recognize the Dove when he passed it coming to visit us.

It became his "Beacon in the Sky." As soon as he saw the Dove, he would start yelling excitedly, "Papa, Gammaw," knowing he was almost at our house. As the years went by, he shared this excitement with his younger sisters, Tracy and Candice.

Today, our grandchildren are teenagers, and now they call us on their cell phone to let us know "we're at the Dove." Whenever we pass the Dove, we think of our grandchildren.

David and Barbara Golub

(Left to right) Tracy, Candice, and Shaun Golub.
Courtesy Barbara Golub

When I was in grade school, I looked forward to our holiday trips to Marion, Kentucky, to see my grandparents, cousins, aunts, and uncles. It was a four-hour trip, which at that age, seemed like 12 hours. The only drawback was the unfortunate problem of car sickness.

Each year my brother and sister were sure to point out the exact spot where I had gotten sick as we made our annual treks. This would inevitably initiate another stop for nausea's sake. On the way to Marion, my only hope for relief was when we hit the ferry that crossed the Ohio River; this was my signal that we were almost there.

Likewise, the problem reared its ugly head on the trip back home to St. Louis. As I sat on the hump in the middle of the back seat, I'd try to lean on my brother or sister, hoping to fall asleep. I remember feeling too energetic to fall asleep and also afraid of hearing those familiar words my brother and sister would occasionally blurt out, "Don't touch me!"

I especially remember one trip home, after what seemed like days in the car, my dad was getting extremely agitated by my asking, "Are we close to home yet?" My mom excitedly said, "Vicki, look! There's the West County Dove! That's the mall we go to, so whenever you see that you'll know we're 15 minutes from home."

Sure enough, I timed it – after all, that was all I had to do! It was a little over 15 minutes from when I saw the Dove until I reached my house. My dad was thrilled with the symbol from that moment on. Thereafter every trip we made to and from Marion, he never had to hear me whine, "Are we there yet?" I still remember straining to see out the window to catch a glimpse of the Dove and then I'd announce, "There's the Dove! We're close to home." Of course, my brother and sister always replied, "Shut up." Then they nudged me to get off of them as I watched the Dove out the window. It's always been a "home" symbol to me. Even as I got older, I'd see the Dove and know I was close to home.

Vicki Brown

I have fond memories of the Dove from my childhood. My family would always meet other family members and friends for weekend float/camping trips very early in the morning at the Dove at West County Center. We would meet there because it was so convenient for everyone, no matter where in St. Louis each person lived. We lived in Fenton at the time, and as a child, the Dove seemed so far away as we anxiously awaited our destination.

It is somewhat ironic to me that I now live directly behind the newly renovated Westfield Shoppingtown West County off of Ballas Road. My family now awaits the Dove's return, waiting for it to "fly back to its perch!"

Thank you for writing this book – I think most St. Louisans will get a kick out of reading Dove stories!

Elizabeth Cowie

Recently I drove past the construction site for the new mall with my grandsons, Zachary (eight) and Nathan (six). Nathan asked if the Dove would be back after they finished, because it "has meaning." When I asked him what it meant, he said, "It means we're almost to Mima's house!"

Helen Yeager

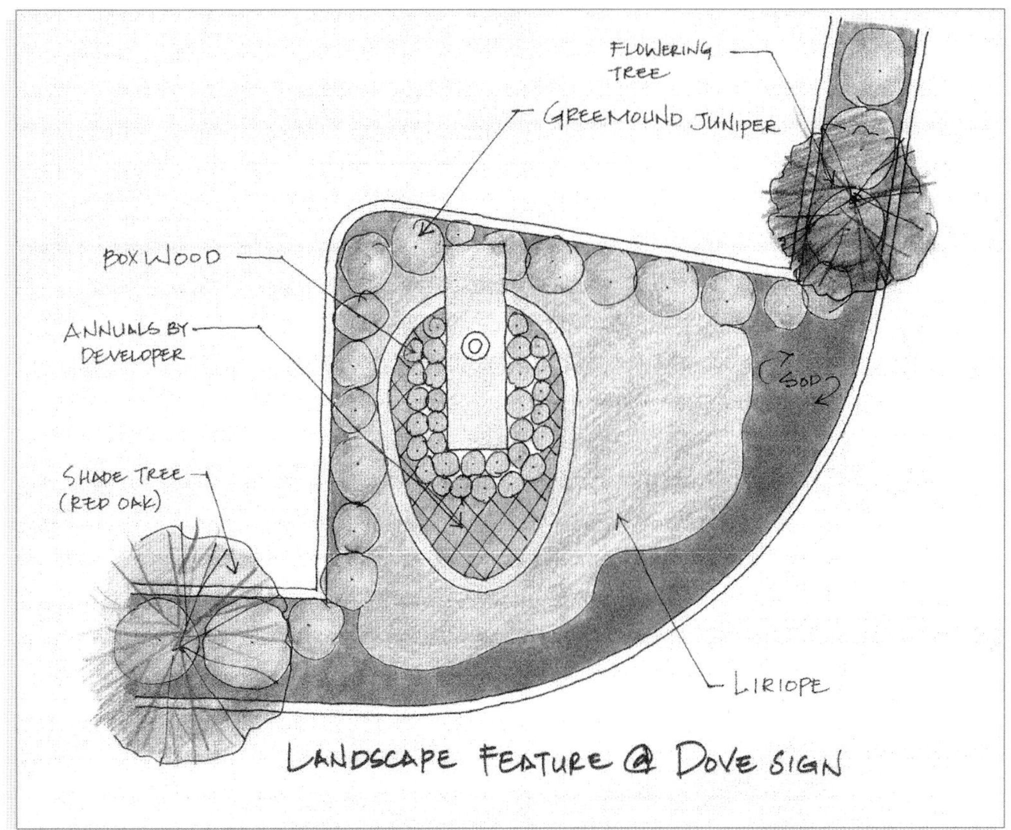

Aerial view of new "nest" for the Dove, 2002.
Courtesy Westfield Shoppingtown West County and City of Des Peres

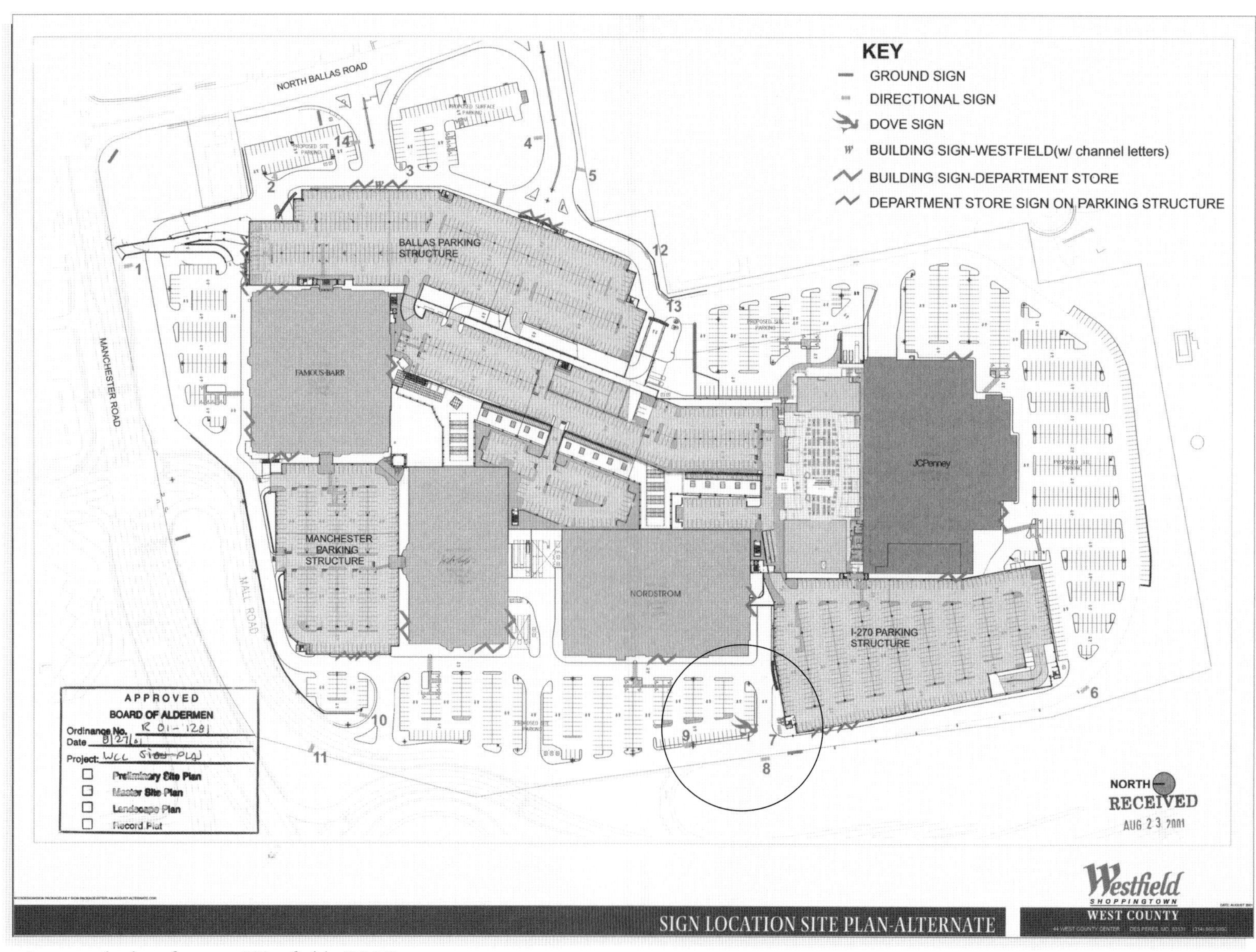

Approved plan for new Westfield, 2002.
Courtesy Westfield Shoppingtown West County and City of Des Peres

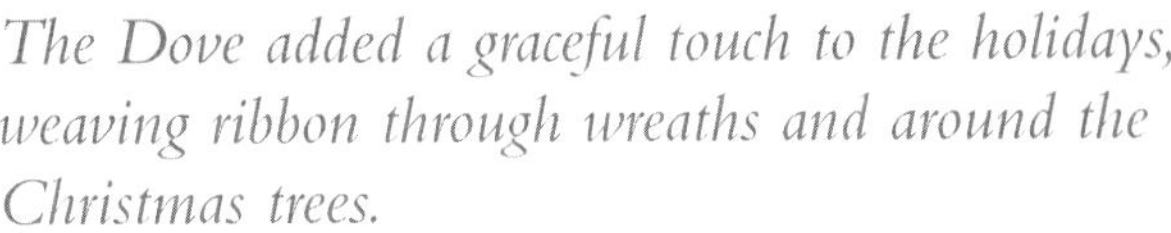

The Dove added a graceful touch to the holidays, weaving ribbon through wreaths and around the Christmas trees.
Courtesy Westfield Shoppingtown West County and Jennifer Petrowsky

The Easter Bunny was a welcome visitor at West County.
Courtesy Westfield Shoppingtown West County and Jennifer Petrowsky

Chapter 6

The Beat Goes On–Other Dove Tales

Under the Dove was the perfect spot for the birding group of the Webster Groves Nature Study Society to meet before starting their weekly birding trips.

Marjorie Richardson

This chapter includes a variety of remembrances. Writers submitted memories of friendship, adventure, and travel that involved the Dove. These unique submissions offer readers a perspective that extends as far south as Florida and far beyond our Missouri border to the north. As these stories came in, it was evident that this book needed to be written. Under the Dove has offered a voice to those individuals who recognize the significance of this majestic symbol.

The Dove enabled two boys to begin a friendship as youngsters that continues today as freshmen at two different universities. My son, Will, met Adam in the fifth grade. The boys shared a love of athletics and good jokes!

Adam's family lived in South County and we lived in Clayton. His mother taught in Clayton, so her son attended school there. Weekends presented a challenge in arranging for the boys to spend time together, and there were many phone calls to make arrangements.

The Dove seemed to be the central meeting spot between us, and the friendship was well worth the effort. Often we had our family in the car, waiting with doors open in the parking lot for the other family to arrive. As I reflect on this arrangement, it certainly proved to be convenient. I never did make it to Adam's house, but grew quite familiar with the drive to the Dove, until eventually his family moved to Clayton.

The Dove enabled this relationship to develop. Today, our families continue to stay in touch, and the long distance phone bills reflect the closeness that continues for the boys as they weather the trials of college life!

Judy Goodman

I was a new driver at 16 years old when we lived by Hampton Village near Hampton and Chippewa. My best friend and I would take the bus to Crestwood Plaza, but when we really wanted to "step out," we would venture as far as the "mall with the Dove." It was a huge deal to drive all the way to the mall. I remember one day begging for the car to drive there with my best friend and getting the typical response from my parents – "No!"

My older brother had a new Dodge Dart that was a bit complicated to drive. It had a button on the dashboard to push instead of a gearshift. After listening to my whining about wanting to go shopping, *he actually offered to let us take his new car to the Dove Mall!*

I was so excited I almost forgot to listen to his driving instructions. We soon set out for the mall, taking the old Highway 66 to 270. I gripped the steering wheel so tightly that my knuckles ached. In my nervousness, I focused on the road in front of me, feeling certain that I knew the way to the mall.

Eventually my friend and I began asking one another, "Did you see the Dove yet? Have you seen the Dove?" Over and over we asked, then eventually we began to wonder if we missed it in our zeal to be attentive to the road ahead.

When we saw a sign greeting us, "Welcome to Alton, Illinois," we knew we had *definitely* missed the Dove! We had traveled nearly 50 miles beyond our destination! By the time we turned around and found the mall, it was time to return home.

It was an unforgettable experience that still makes me smile, even today.

Maryann Vitale

I was in college in Nashville, Tennessee, while West County Center was being built in the 1960's. When I left St. Louis, the Manchester Drive-In was still there. I knew the center would be built, but had no idea that there would be a lighted Dove.

Early in June of 1969, my family drove to Nashville for my graduation and then moved me back from Belmont University. As you can imagine, I accumulated quite a bit of junk during my stay at college. My roommate's father insisted on giving my mother a large milk can that subsequently became wedged between us in the back seat. My parents packed my brother and me into our overloaded station wagon and we headed home for St. Louis.

By the time we reached Manchester Road on Highway 270, it was 2:00 A.M., and I woke up as my father slowed down at the exit. I looked out the window and, much to my amazement, there was an enormous Dove that appeared to be floating in the dark sky. From the angle of the highway, I couldn't see the pole, the parking lot, or the stores – only the Dove. No one else in the car said anything about this phenomenon, so I wondered if I was hallucinating. I didn't want to upset my parents by announcing my vision. After all, they had just spent a lot of money to educate me. Would they wonder what went wrong?

When we were on Manchester Road, I was relieved to discover that the Dove didn't seem to be following me after all, so I risked taking a look back. At that point I could see that the drive-in had become a mall with a lighted Dove on a pole. I was not hallucinating after all!

Despite my unexpected encounter with the Dove, it has become one of my favorite landmarks. Once I no longer worried about my mental state as a distressed college graduate, I grew very fond of the Dove. I am delighted that it is returning to its home!

Lynn K. Silence

The Dove awaiting a face-lift at Signcrafters, Inc.
Photo by Gary Lang

The Dove with the face removed, awaiting renovation by Signcrafters, Inc.
Photo by Gary Lang

I am a member of the Assumption Greek Orthodox Church on Des Peres Road, which has been located near Highway 270 and Manchester for 20 years. I volunteer to help with two Greek festivals we celebrate – one in May and one in September. My job is to give directions to people who call, and I would be lost without the Dove! I use it as a landmark and begin by asking callers, "Do you know where the West County Dove is on 270 and Manchester?" Nine times out of 10, they reply, "Oh yes, now I know." It makes my job very easy after that.

Thanks to the West County Dove, many visitors have been guided to our festivals and to our weekly luncheons. God bless the Dove and anyone sharing a story about it. We will be happy when it is restored and resumes its position as a landmark beacon in the sky!

Maria Magafas

How many lights are in the Dove?

•

a. 11

b. 22

c. 33

•

There are 22 mercury vapor lights in the Dove, each one is 175 watts.

As a pleasure traveler and shopping center enthusiast, I've been to over 200 malls across the United States and Canada. But I was particularly struck by the unusual architecture of the St. Louis area older malls with the huge copulas atop the roofs of the Famous-Barr stores.

Then I saw *the Dove!* There it was in all its glory in the shadow of Plaza Frontenac and the Galleria as well. I went in for a few minutes to check out the music store during my visit in 1996 and learned that they were going to add a Nordstrom at Westfield Shoppingtown West County.

I told my mom, "We've got to go back when it opens!" Well, we're planning our entire vacation around Westfield Shoppingtown West County grand reopening in September, and believe me, it will be worth it!

Michael Soto

Growing up in North County, a trip to West County Center was a treat! When mom would tell my sisters and me that we were going shopping, we always excitedly asked, "The mall with the Dove?" It seemed like such a long trip back then. Our favorite spot to shop was the Mod Shop in Famous-Barr. Then, of course, we always enjoyed a cup of their French onion soup!

Joanne Noyes

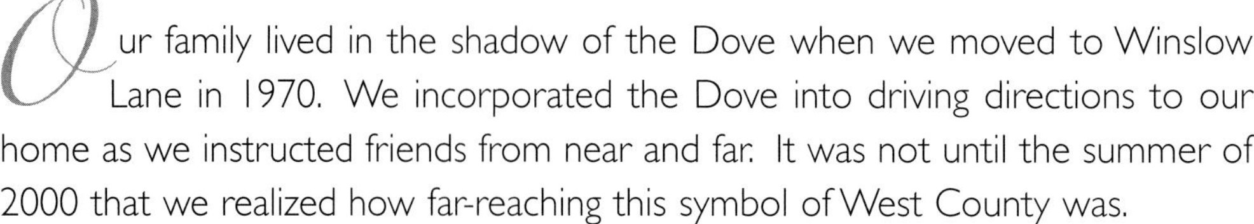

Our family lived in the shadow of the Dove when we moved to Winslow Lane in 1970. We incorporated the Dove into driving directions to our home as we instructed friends from near and far. It was not until the summer of 2000 that we realized how far-reaching this symbol of West County was.

We purchased a small parcel of land on Anastasia Island near St. Augustine, Florida – nearly 1000 miles from St. Louis. Our realtor, Jane, said she didn't know much about the Midwest, but her best friend, who now lives at the beach, was from St. Louis. So, true to St. Louis tradition, we quizzed her as to what part of St. Louis her friend was from. She replied, "Well, all I know is that she lived near some big Dove." Jane was dumbfounded that we knew exactly where her friend was from and that she was surely a former neighbor of ours!

Alyce Finder

I am so happy that the Dove will return to the Westfield Shoppingtown West County. My memories of the Dove began when we moved to Kirkwood and the center first opened. Our extended family lived in Wisconsin and came to this area to visit each year. Our directions were to "look for the Dove at West County Center and the next exit will be Big Bend [this was before we had the Dougherty Ferry Exit]" No one ever got lost because the "sign of the Dove" was a perfect landmark. Thank you for keeping our memories alive.

Carol Ann Miller

Under the Dove was a great meeting spot for the Missouri Association of Playwrights.
Courtesy Virginia Engel

The last time I met someone under the Dove I had several boxes of props and costumes for the Missouri Association of Playwrights (MAP), which was going to show my one-act play "Pharoah Forgotten," and they needed those things.

It happened to be the day I was to audition for a commercial for the Missouri Lottery. To save time, I wore an old-fashioned western costume for the audition. I felt stupid in that outfit, unloading the boxes from my trunk to the MAP car in the middle of the day; however, I consoled myself, hoping anyone looking would think I was going to a Halloween party, since it was about that time of the year.

I felt even better about it after the audition when they called to tell me that I was hired for the part. Oh yes, I say that the white Dove is very special to me and brings back what turned out to be a happy memory.

Virginia Engel

Bird Call

The big white dove is calling
It's time for "West County Malling"
Famous, Penney's, Nordstrom
And the stores in between
I've proclaimed
My new name
To be THE SHOPPING QUEEN!

DONNA DALESSANDRO

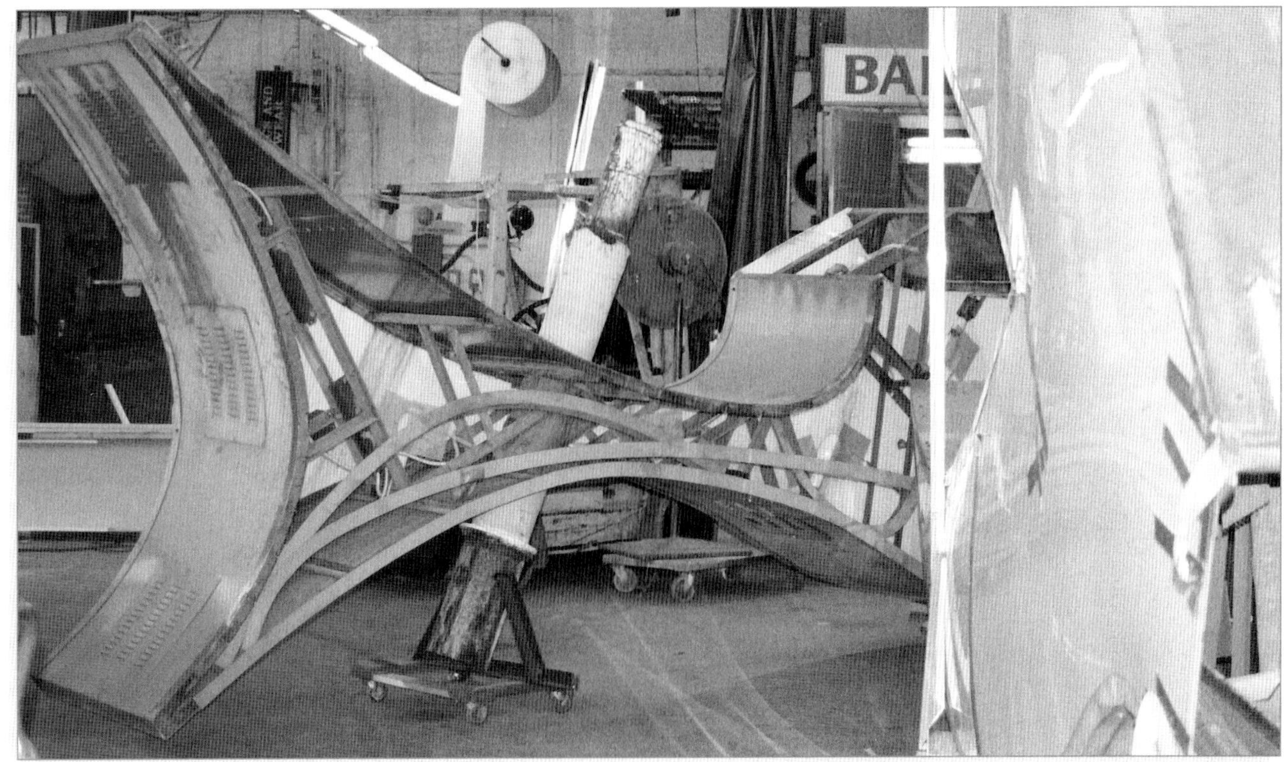

Afterword

Interviews for this book revealed surprising information that many people may not know about the City of Des Peres. For instance, the people involved in its local government and commerce worked very closely together. Many communities seem to encounter somewhat of a tug-of-war as a result of divisions in values and beliefs. On the contrary, in Des Peres the government has developed a "culture" about the landscape of the city that has stood firm for many generations.

This consistency results from the fact that many family names appear for generations in the city's history. When Des Peres began to organize its government in the late 1800's, it wanted to preserve its identity. Des Peres is French for "of the Fathers," which is probably a credit to the Jesuit missionaries who established a temporary settlement in the area during the 1700's. However, when German immigrants settled there a century later, Des Peres became recognized as the "City of Flowers" because of the hundreds of acres devoted to growing flowers for commercial use.

When times changed, the focus on the quality of residential neighborhoods remained a priority. The residents voted for a one-cent sales tax, allowing the city to provide superior fire and police protection and other public services, including an outstanding community center. Des Peres has been able to generously provide for its residents because of the millions that this small tax generates.

Writing this book has allowed me to appreciate this community in a new way. I am not from Des Peres, and I typically refer to it simply as West County, as though it is part of a region of St. Louis. I had not thought much about its identity as a city until recently.

Writing a book about the Dove indicates that the pride in it extends beyond the city boundaries of Des Peres. Anyone who travels Highway 270 can identify with it, no matter what community they live in.

Initially, I was fascinated with the Dove, and the stories that needed to be told. However, I began to discover more about the Dove and the community around it. When planners began their work on the center and the Dove in the 1960's, no one expected it to soar to such notoriety over the years. It is not like any other shopping center sign, and area residents beyond the boundaries of Des Peres take pride in it.

Because of the strong, consistent leadership in local government, the Dove became a regional landmark. Unbelievable growth is evident when driving east or west on Manchester. However, growth is not nearly as evident when driving between Highway 44 and Ladue Road on Highway 270. As a result, the Dove has no other distractions that draw viewers away from its perch on Highway 270. What makes it remarkable is its location, and the fact that there are no other signs around it. This was deliberate on the part of local government.

The proud tradition of these hard-working men and women was a common theme throughout the research for this book. When Westfield first purchased the outdated mall, their offices in California had a difficult time understanding why the Dove was so important. After many hours of negotiations, it became evident that the community stood firm in wanting the Dove to remain as the local icon.

This simple decision was not necessarily easy to convey to Westfield, yet this firm stance is one that all of St. Louis celebrates as the Dove returns to the new center. The Dove will enable Des Peres to move into a new century while preserving a part of past tradition. After all, the Dove was the identifier for decades, and now it can continue in that role long after the new Westfield is complete.

Another example of the way Des Peres values its residents was evident in the decision to hold Westfield within its original property line. No family would be displaced as a result of the new construction. Many people wondered how such a large, new mall could be built on such a seemingly tiny lot. Yet this was a decision that preserved residential homes and challenged the best of architects. The result is a tasteful, high-profile shopping center.

Gathering information for this book was similar to the task of an investigative reporter. One interview seemed to naturally lead to another, then another. Two pressing questions were: Who designed the Dove? Who made the original sign? It was very satisfying to answer these and other questions that arose – even the simple ones.

The surprising aspect of writing was discovering the "story behind the story" in each interview. Learning about the personal lives of the people who pieced together the history was so much a part of how they performed in their work functions. They shared information that revealed their character – their dedication and persistence. They did what they believed was in the best interest of the center, consumers, and city residents. The leadership roles they assumed reflected their willingness to serve others rather than to bring attention to themselves. While this may not be true for all elected officials and management, it certainly appeared to be evident in those interviewed for this book.

Reflecting on the work involved in writing about the Dove brought both satisfaction and a bit of worry. Satisfaction came from knowing the questions that seemed important were answered. Worry came from wondering if anyone was left out or was misrepresented. If this happened, please forgive me. In either case, I continue to be grateful for those who worked hard to preserve the Dove and those who treasure it.

The author poses between the top and bottom sections of the Dove as it awaits renovations at Signcrafters, Inc.
Photo by Gary Lang

Contributors

Mary Bailey
Jean Marie Baker
Vicki Brown
Barb Buren
Peggy Cooper
Elizabeth Cowie
Danny Daniels
Donna Dalessandro
Andre Edwards
Rachel Elliott
Virginia Engel
Lauren Erger
Krystal Farley
Mary Fava
Alyce Finder
Mary Flotron
Christine Foster
David and Barb Golub
Judy Goodman
Trish Washburn Gunby
Carolyn Hampel
Margaret Hoeft
Daniel Hrdlicka
Audrey Lang
Nancy Latt
Dorothy (Cimaglia) Liberton
Maria Magafas
Michelle Graham Martin
Mike Mertzlufft
Carol Ann Miller
Wes Neu
Joanne Noyes
Judy Olsen
Marion Pleis
Rebecca Randolph
Marjorie Richardson
Pat Rush
Bill and Marge Ryan
Laurie Schack
Lynn K. Silence
Randy Smith
Harold B. Sykora
Michael Soto
Maryann Vitale
Pam (McLean) Wingbermuehle
Sally Wheeler
Helen Yaeger

Special Contributors

Dan Buck, *Host – Show Me St. Louis and the KTRS Morning Show*
Sharon Burkhardt, *former Mayor – City of Des Peres*
Ted Drewes, *Ted Drewes Frozen Custard*
Jody Griggs, *former Mayor – City of Des Peres*
Rick Lahr, *Mayor – City of Des Peres*
Jim Morhmann, *Signcrafters, Inc.*
Duane T. Nicks, *Chairman of the Board – Famous-Barr*
Dean Percival, *General Sign Company*
Jennifer (O'Keefe) Petrowsky, former *General Manager – Westfield Shoppingtown West County*
Sean Phillips, *Associate Regional Marketing Director – Westfield Corporation*
Joe Thaler, *Designer of the Dove*
A. William Trucksess, *President - Philadelphia Sign Company*
Scott Vallee, *General Manager – Westfield Shoppingtown West County*
Elaine Viets, *Mystery Writer*
Buzz Westfall, *St. Louis County Executive*
Wendy Wiese, *Radio Personality 550 KTRS*
Nan Wyatt, *Co-host Total Information AM*
Anita Yeckel, *State Senator, District 1*
Glenn Zimmerman, *Weather Department, KTVI Fox 2*